The reform'd coquet; or, memoirs of Amoranda. A surprising novel. By Mrs. Davys.

Mary Davys

The reform'd coquet; or, memoirs of Amoranda. A surprising novel. By Mrs. Davys.
Davys, Mary
ESTCID: T008503
Reproduction from British Library
Preface signed: Mary Davys.
Dublin : printed by M. Rhames, for R. Gunne, 1735.
v,[3],99,[1]p. ; 12°

Eighteenth Century
Collections Online
Print Editions

Gale ECCO Print Editions

Relive history with *Eighteenth Century Collections Online*, now available in print for the independent historian and collector. This series includes the most significant English-language and foreign-language works printed in Great Britain during the eighteenth century, and is organized in seven different subject areas including literature and language; medicine, science, and technology; and religion and philosophy. The collection also includes thousands of important works from the Americas.

The eighteenth century has been called "The Age of Enlightenment." It was a period of rapid advance in print culture and publishing, in world exploration, and in the rapid growth of science and technology – all of which had a profound impact on the political and cultural landscape. At the end of the century the American Revolution, French Revolution and Industrial Revolution, perhaps three of the most significant events in modern history, set in motion developments that eventually dominated world political, economic, and social life.

In a groundbreaking effort, Gale initiated a revolution of its own: digitization of epic proportions to preserve these invaluable works in the largest online archive of its kind. Contributions from major world libraries constitute over 175,000 original printed works. Scanned images of the actual pages, rather than transcriptions, recreate the works ***as they first appeared.***

Now for the first time, these high-quality digital scans of original works are available via print-on-demand, making them readily accessible to libraries, students, independent scholars, and readers of all ages.

For our initial release we have created seven robust collections to form one the world's most comprehensive catalogs of 18th century works.

Initial Gale ECCO Print Editions collections include:

History and Geography

Rich in titles on English life and social history, this collection spans the world as it was known to eighteenth-century historians and explorers. Titles include a wealth of travel accounts and diaries, histories of nations from throughout the world, and maps and charts of a world that was still being discovered. Students of the War of American Independence will find fascinating accounts from the British side of conflict.

Social Science
Delve into what it was like to live during the eighteenth century by reading the first-hand accounts of everyday people, including city dwellers and farmers, businessmen and bankers, artisans and merchants, artists and their patrons, politicians and their constituents. Original texts make the American, French, and Industrial revolutions vividly contemporary.

Medicine, Science and Technology
Medical theory and practice of the 1700s developed rapidly, as is evidenced by the extensive collection, which includes descriptions of diseases, their conditions, and treatments. Books on science and technology, agriculture, military technology, natural philosophy, even cookbooks, are all contained here.

Literature and Language
Western literary study flows out of eighteenth-century works by Alexander Pope, Daniel Defoe, Henry Fielding, Frances Burney, Denis Diderot, Johann Gottfried Herder, Johann Wolfgang von Goethe, and others. Experience the birth of the modern novel, or compare the development of language using dictionaries and grammar discourses.

Religion and Philosophy
The Age of Enlightenment profoundly enriched religious and philosophical understanding and continues to influence present-day thinking. Works collected here include masterpieces by David Hume, Immanuel Kant, and Jean-Jacques Rousseau, as well as religious sermons and moral debates on the issues of the day, such as the slave trade. The Age of Reason saw conflict between Protestantism and Catholicism transformed into one between faith and logic -- a debate that continues in the twenty-first century.

Law and Reference
This collection reveals the history of English common law and Empire law in a vastly changing world of British expansion. Dominating the legal field is the *Commentaries of the Law of England* by Sir William Blackstone, which first appeared in 1765. Reference works such as almanacs and catalogues continue to educate us by revealing the day-to-day workings of society.

Fine Arts
The eighteenth-century fascination with Greek and Roman antiquity followed the systematic excavation of the ruins at Pompeii and Herculaneum in southern Italy; and after 1750 a neoclassical style dominated all artistic fields. The titles here trace developments in mostly English-language works on painting, sculpture, architecture, music, theater, and other disciplines. Instructional works on musical instruments, catalogs of art objects, comic operas, and more are also included.

The BiblioLife Network

This project was made possible in part by the BiblioLife Network (BLN), a project aimed at addressing some of the huge challenges facing book preservationists around the world. The BLN includes libraries, library networks, archives, subject matter experts, online communities and library service providers. We believe every book ever published should be available as a high-quality print reproduction; printed on-demand anywhere in the world. This insures the ongoing accessibility of the content and helps generate sustainable revenue for the libraries and organizations that work to preserve these important materials.

The following book is in the "public domain" and represents an authentic reproduction of the text as printed by the original publisher. While we have attempted to accurately maintain the integrity of the original work, there are sometimes problems with the original work or the micro-film from which the books were digitized. This can result in minor errors in reproduction. Possible imperfections include missing and blurred pages, poor pictures, markings and other reproduction issues beyond our control. Because this work is culturally important, we have made it available as part of our commitment to protecting, preserving, and promoting the world's literature.

GUIDE TO FOLD-OUTS MAPS and OVERSIZED IMAGES

The book you are reading was digitized from microfilm captured over the past thirty to forty years. Years after the creation of the original microfilm, the book was converted to digital files and made available in an online database.

In an online database, page images do not need to conform to the size restrictions found in a printed book. When converting these images back into a printed bound book, the page sizes are standardized in ways that maintain the detail of the original. For large images, such as fold-out maps, the original page image is split into two or more pages

Guidelines used to determine how to split the page image follows:

- Some images are split vertically; large images require vertical and horizontal splits.
- For horizontal splits, the content is split left to right.
- For vertical splits, the content is split from top to bottom.
- For both vertical and horizontal splits, the image is processed from top left to bottom right.

THE REFORM'D COQUET;
OR,
MEMOIRS
OF
AMORANDA.

A Surprising
NOVEL.

By Mrs. *DAVYS.*

Nil moror quam pueriliter, modo utiliter.
                                        Erasm

DUBLIN:
Printed by M. Rhames,
For R. Gunne, Bookseller in *Capel-street.*
MDCCXXXV.

TO THE
LADIES
OF
GREAT BRITAIN.

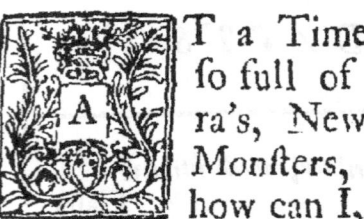T a Time when the Town is so full of Masquerades, Opera's, New Plays, Conjurors, Monsters, and feign'd Devils; how can I, Ladies, expect you to throw away an Hour upon the less agreeable Amusement my *Coquet* can give you? But she who has assurance to write, has certainly the vanity of expecting to be read: All Authors see a Beauty in their own Compositions, which perhaps no body else can find; as Mothers think their own Offspring amiable, how deficient so-vere Nature has been to them. But what-
ever

ever my Faults may be, my Design is good, and hope you *British* Ladies will accordingly encourage it.

If I have here touch'd a young Lady's Vanity and Levity, it was to show her how Beautiful she is without those Blots, which certainly stain the Mind, and stamp Deformity where the greatest Beauties would shine, were they banish'd. I believe every body will join with my Opinion, that the *English* Ladies are the most accomplish'd Women in the World; that generally speaking, their Behaviour is so exact, that even Envy itself cannot strike at their Conduct: But even you yourselves must own, that there are some few among you of a different Stamp, who change their Gold for Dross, and barter the highest Perfections for the lowest Weaknesses. Would but this latter sort endeavour as much to act like Angels, as they do to look like them, the Men instead of Reproaches, would heap them with Praises, and their cold Indifference would be turn'd to Idolatry. But who can forsake a Fault, till they are convinc'd they are guilty? Vanity is a lurking subtile Thief, that works itself insensibly into our Bosoms, and while we declare our dislike to it, know not it is so near us; every body being (as a witty Gentleman has somewhere said) provided with a Racket to strike it from themselves.

The

The Heroine of the following Sheets will tell you the Advantages of a kind friendly Admonition, and when the little Lightnesses of her Mind were removed, she became worthy of Imitation. One little Word of Advice, Ladies, and I have done: When you grow weary of Flattery, and begin to listen to matrimonial Addresses, chuse a Man of fine Sense, as well as a fine Wigg, and let him have some Merit, as well as much Embroidery: This will make Coxcombs give ground, and Men of Sense will equally admire your Conduct with your Beauty. I am,

LADIES,

Your most Devoted,

And most Obedient

Humble Servant,

MARY DAVYS.

THE PREFACE.

DLENESS has so long been an Excuse for Writing, that I am almost ashamed to tell the World it was that, and that only, which produced the following Sheets. Few People are so inconsiderable in Life, but they may at some time do good; and though I must own my Purse is [by a thousand Misfortunes] grown wholly useless to every body, my Pen is at the Service of the Publick, and if it can but make some Impression upon the young unthinking Minds of some of my own Sex, I shall bless my Labour, and reap an unspeakable Satisfaction: But as I have addressed them in another Place, I shall say no more of them here.

I come now to the worthy Gentlemen of Cambridge, from whom I have receiv'd so many Marks of Favour on a thousand Occasions, that my Gratitude is highly concerned how to

make

The PREFACE.

make a due Acknowledgment; and I own their civil, generous, good-natur'd Behaviour towards me, is the only Thing I have now left worth boasting of. When I had written a Sheet or two of this Novel, I communicated my Design to a couple of young Gentlemen, whom I knew to be Men of Taste, and both my Friends; they approved of what I had done, advised me to proceed, then print it by Subscription: Into which Proposal many of the Gentlemen entered, among whom were a good Number of both the grave and the young Clergy, who the World will easily believe had a greater View to Charity than Novelty; and it was not to the Book, but the Author, they subscribed. They knew her to be a Relict of one of their Brotherhood, and one, who [unless Poverty be a Sin] never did any thing to disgrace the Gown; and for those Reasons encouraged all her Undertakings.

But as this Book was writ at Cambridge, I am a little apprehensive some may imagine the Gentlemen had a Hand in it. It would be very hard, if their Humanity to me, should bring an Imputation upon themselves so greatly below their Merit, which I can by no means consent to; and do therefore assure the World, I am not acquainted with one Member of that Worthy and Learned Society of Men, whose Pens are not employed in Things infinitely above any Thing I can pretend to be the Author of: So that I only am accountable for every Fault of my Book; and if it has any Beauties,

The PREFACE.

ties, I claim the Merit of them too. Though I cannot but say, I did once apply myself to a young Genius for a Preface, which he seem'd to decline, and I soon consider'd the Brightness of his Pen would only eclipse the glimmering Light of my own; so called back my Request, and resolved to entertain my Readers with a Pattern, in the Preface, of the same Stuff the following Sheets are made of; which will, I hope, give them an Hour or two of agreeable Amusement. And if they will but be as kind to me, as they have been to many before, they will overlook one little Improbability, because such are to be met with in most Novels, many Plays, and even in Travels themselves. There is a little Story in the Beginning of the Book, of the Courtship of a Boy, which the Reader may, perhaps, think very trifling: But as it is not two Pages long, I beg he will pass it by; and my Excuse for it is, I could not so well shew the early Coquetry of the Lady without it.

THE REFORM'D COQUET;

OR,

Memoirs of *Amoranda*.

THE most Avaricious Scribbler that ever took Pen in hand, had doubtless a view to his Reputation, separate from his Interest. I confess myself a Lover of Money, and yet have the greatest Inclination to please my Readers, but how to do so is a very critical Point, and what more correct Pens than mine have miss'd of. If we divide Mankind into several Classes, we shall meet with as many different Tempers as Faces, only we have the Art of disguising one better than t'other.

The Pedant despises the most elaborate Undertaking, unless it appears in the World with *Greek* and *Latin* Motto's, a Man that would please him, must pore an Age over musty Authors, till his Brains are as worm-eaten as the Books he reads, and his Coversation fit for no body else I have neither Inclination nor Learning enough to hope for his Favour, so lay him aside.

The next I can never hope to please, is the Dogmatical Puppy, who, like a Hedgehog, is wrapt up in his own Opinions, and despises all who want Extravagances to enter into them, but a Man must have a superior share of Pride, who can expect his single Opinion should byass the rest of the Creation: I leave him therefore to pine at his Disappointment, and call upon

the

the busy part of our Species, who are so very intent upon getting Money, that they lose the Pleasure of spending it. I confess, the *Royal Exchange, South-Sea* with a P—x, *Exchange-Alley*, and all Trade in general, are so foreign to my Understanding, that I leave them where I found them, and cast an oblique Glance at the Philosopher, who I take to be a good clever Fellow in his way. But as I am again forced to betray my Ignorance, I know so little of him, that I leave him to his, *No Pleasure, no Pain*; and a thousand other Chimera's while I face about to the Man of Gallantry. Love is a very common Topick, but 'tis withal a very copious one, and would the Poets, Printers and Booksellers, but speak Truth of it, they would own themselves more obliged to that one Subject for their Bread, than all the rest put together. 'Tis there I fix, and the following Sheets are to be filled with the Tale of a fine young Lady.

A certain Knight who lives pretty deep in the Country, had a Father whose vicious Inclinations led him into a thousand Extravagances, whoring and drinking took up a great part of his time, and the rest was spent in gaming, which was his darling Diversion. We have had so many melancholly Instances of the sad Effects of this Vice, that I dare say the Reader will not be surprized if I tell him, this Gentleman in a little time died a Beggar by it, and left the young Baronet no more than his Honour to live upon. Some years before the old Gentleman died, the young one married a Lady clandestinely, whose Fortune was then all their Support, and by whom he had one Daughter, now seven years of age, and for whom I will borrow the Name of *Amoranda* Sir *John S———d*, her Father, had a younger Brother bred an *East India* Merchant, his Success abroad was so very great, that it qualified him for shewing large Bounty at Home, and as he thought nothing so despicable as Honour and Poverty join'd, he was resolved to set his elder Brother above Contempt, and make him shine like the Head of so antient a Family, in order to which, he first redeem'd all the Land his Father had mortgaged for money to fling away, then repurchased

chased all he had sold, till at last he had settled the Knight in a quiet Possession of that Estate, which had for many Ages devolved from Father to Son, but, as he was exceeding fond of his young Niece, settled the whole upon her, in case her Father died without a Son, not making the least reserve in favour of himself. When he had, with the highest Satisfaction, done a Deed of so much Goodness and Generosity, he left the Family he had just made happy, and went again in pursuit of his Merchandise, in the mean time, *Amoranda*, who was a little Angel for Beauty, was extreamly admir'd, no less for that, than for a sprightly Wit, which her younger years promis'd. If we trace humane Nature through all the stages of Life, we shall find those dawnings of the Passions in Children, which riper years bring to the highest perfection; and a Child, rightly considered, may give us a very great guess at his Temper, when he comes to be a Man. An Instance of this we have in the young Creature already named, who had, 'tis true, all the Beauties of her Sex; but then she had the seeds of their Pride and Vanity too. *Amoranda* was no sooner told she was pretty than she believ'd it, and listen'd with pleasure to those who said her Eyes were Diamonds, her Cheeks Roses, her Skin Alabaster, her Lips Coral, and her Hair *Cupid*'s Nets, which were to ensnare and catch all Mankind.

This made an early Impression upon the Mind of young *Amoranda*, and she now began to think as much in favour of herself as it was possible for others to do. Her Babies were thrown by with scorn, and the time that should have dress'd them was spent at the Lookingglass, dressing herself, admiring all those Graces with which she was now sure she was surrounded, her Father's Visiters were no longer to use her with their wonted Freedom, but she told them with an Air of growing Pride, she expected to be called Madam as well as her Mamma, and she was not so much a Child as they would make her. Whilst she was in the midst of her grand Airs, a little Boy came in who used to call her Wife, and running to her, got his little Arms about her Neck to kiss her, as he used to do. But *Amoranda*, who was now resolv'd to be a Woman, thrust him from

he

her with the utmost Contempt, and bad him see her no more. The poor Boy, not us'd to such Behaviour, stood staring at her in great Surprize at the occasion of all this, but being a Boy of some Spirit, tho' not capable of a real Passion, he said, Madam, you need not be so proud, I have got a Prettier than you for my Wife, and love her better than I do you by half, and I will never come near you again. Saying thus, away he went to make his Complaints at home. When *Amoranda* saw him gone, and with a design to go to another, the whole Woman gather'd in her Soul, and she fell into a violent Passion of Tears; the Thoughts of having another preferr'd to her was intolerable, and seeing the Boy go off with Insults, gave her a very sensible Mortification. Resentment flash'd in her Eyes, and her Breast heav'd with such Agonies, as the whole Sex feel when they meet with Contempt from a slighting Lover. Her Mother, who was as full of Mirth, as she was of Grief upon this cutting occasion, said to her, Why, *Amoranda*, did you send away your Spouse, if you are angry now he is gone; My Spouse? *cry'd the young incensed*, I scorn the little unmannerly Brat, he shall never be my Spouse what! tell me to my Face he lik'd another better! but I know who the saucy Jackanapes meant, and if ever she comes here again I'll send her to him: I hate them both, and so I'll tell 'em; who can bear such an Affront? I shall never be easy till I am revenged of 'em. Here was Pride, Jealousy, and Revenge, kindled in the Breast of a Child; and as Princes love the Treason, though they hate the Traitor, so Women like the Love, though they despise the Lover.

Poor Amoranda! what will be thy Fate?
So soon to like the Love, the Lover hate!

Her Behaviour, however, gave good diversion to her Father and Mother; and under that mistaken Notion, of every thing looking well in a Child, she was encouraged in many things, which she herself would probably have been asham'd of, had there been time given for Reason to play its part, and help to guard her Actions: most Mothers are fond of seeing their Children Women

Women before their time, but forget it makes themselves look old.

Vanity, which is most Women's *Foible*, might be overlook'd or wink'd at, would it live alone, but alack! it loves a long train of Attendants, and calls in Pride, Affectation, Ill-nature, and often Ill-manners too, for its Companions. A Woman thus surrounded, should be avoided with the same care a Man would shun his evil Genius; 'tis marrying a complication of the worst Diseases.

I remember, when I was a Child, a Gentleman came to make love to a Sister I had, who was a good clever Girl both in Sense and Person, but as Women are never perfect, she had her Failings among the rest, and mightily affected a scornful Toss with her Head, which was so disagreeable, after a few Visits, to her Lover, that he came no more. My Father, a little surpriz'd at his going so abruptly off, and being loth to lose so advantageous a Match for his Daughter, went to enquire after his Reasons, which, when he heard, he told the Gentleman he thought 'em very trifling. No, Sir, *said he*, a Woman who will throw up her Head at me before Marriage, will [ten to one] break mine after it. I know, *continued he*, if a Woman be dishonourably attack'd, her Scorn is needful, her Pride requisite, but a Man of equal or superior Fortune, who has no Views but hers and his own Happiness, ought to be receiv'd with another Air; and if ever I marry, I will have at least a prospect of good Usage. Thus the foolish Girl lost a much better Husband than she got, by thinking her Pride added to her Charms, and gave new Graces to her Behaviour.

Amoranda was now in the ninth year of her Age, six more I leap over, and take her again in her fifteenth, during which time her Father died, and left her a finish'd Beauty and Coquet. I might here have said Fortune too, being sole Heiress to Three Thousand Pounds a year. her Mother and Uncle were left her Guardians, but the former being a Lady of an infirm Constitution, the Grief of losing a tender good Husband made such considerable Additions to her former Weakness, that in less than half a year she died

B too

too, and left poor *Amoranda* open to all the Temptations that Youth, Beauty, Fortune, and flashy Wit could expose her to. Her Uncle but just come from the *Indies*, and whose Business would not admit of his going into the Country, had once a mind to send for her up to Town, but he consider'd *London* a Place of too many Temptations, and since she was willing to stay in the Country, he was resolv'd she should, but desired she would let him send down one to supply his place, and take care of her in his stead. During this *Interregnum*, *Amoranda* was address'd by all the Country round, from the old Justice to the young Rake, and I dare say, my Reader will believe she was a Toast in every House for ten Parishes round. The very Excrescences of her Temper were now become Graces, and it was not possible for one single Fault to be join'd to Three Thousand Pounds a year, her *Levee* was daily crowded with almost all sorts, and she [pleased to be admir'd] though she lov'd none, was complaisant to all. Among a considerable number of Admirers, Lord *Lofty* was one, who had so great a value for his dear self, that he could hardly be persuaded any Woman had Merit enough to deserve the smallest of his Favours, much less the great one of being his Partner for Life. however, he thought *Amoranda* a pretty Play-thing, a young unthinking Girl, left at present to her own Conduct, and if he could draw her in to give him an hour's diversion now and then, he should meet her with some pleasure, if not [though he did not despair] he was her humble Servant, and had no farther design upon her One day he came to see her so early in the morning, that she was hardly up when he came, but sent down word, as soon as she could get herself into a Dress fit to appear before his Lordship she would wait upon him While *Amoranda* was dressing, my Lord took a Walk in the Garden, either to amuse himself with variety of pleasing Objects, or to meditate afresh upon his present Undertaking He walk'd with the utmost pleasure among the Jessamine and Orange Trees At the end of the Walk was a Seat, over which was a fine painted Roof representing the Rape of *Hellen*, on which he gaz'd with some Admiration, and could not

for

forbear comparing *Amoranda* to her, not thinking the whole Scene unlike his own Design. After he had viewed this fine Piece, he happen'd to cast his Eye a little forward, and saw a Paper lye upon the Ground, which he went and took up, finding it directed to *Amoranda* in a Woman's hand: he was not long persuading himself to open it, by which you will believe my Lord a Man of none of the strictest Honour, however, he read it, and found it thus.

IF *the Advice of a Stranger can be of any import, I beg of you, good Madam, to take Care of Lord* Lofty, *who carries nothing but Ruin to our whole Sex: Believe me, who have too fatally experienced him, his whole Design upon you is to make you miserable, and if you fall into his Snare after so fair a Warning, no-body but yourself deserves the Blame.*

This Letter put my Lord into a very thoughtful Posture, and he now began to fear his Hopes of *Amoranda* were at an End; the hand he knew, and acknowledged the Person who writ it a much better Painter than him he had been so lately admiring, since she had drawn him so much to the Life. My Lord was a Man of the best Assurance in *England*, yet he began to fear his Courage would not hold out to face *Amoranda* any more, and was just resolving to leave the Garden, and go home, when he saw her coming towards him, he shuffl'd the Letter into his pocket, and with a Countenance half confounded went to meet her. Good-morrow, my Lord [*said* Amoranda *with the gayest Air*] how are we to construe those early Sallies of yours? not to Love, I suppose; because Mr *Congreve* tells us, *A Contemplative Lover can no more leave his Bed in a morning, than he can sleep in it.*

Madam, *said my Lord* [*who began to gather Courage from her Behaviour*] a contemplative Lover has some respite from his pain, but a restless one has none, I hope you will believe I am one of this last sort, and am come to look for my Repose where I lost it. Fye! fye! my Lord, how you talk! *said* Amoranda, you're a Man of so much Gallantry there's no dealing with you. Come, *said she*, take my Hand, and let us go to the Fish-Ponds,

I have

I have ordered the Tackling to be carry'd down before us, we'll try if we can find any Sport this morning. Madam, *said my Lord*, every thing is Diversion in your Company, and if you can captivate your Fish as fast as you do those of your own Species, your Ponds will be in a little time quite ruin'd.

O! my Lord, *said Amoranda*, if I catch too many of either sort, I have a very good way of disposing of them.

After what manner? *said my Lord*. Why, *said she*, one I throw into the Water again, and t'other may consume in his own Flames. Madam, *said my Lord*, he's a cruel Deity who is pleas'd with nothing but the Life of his Worshippers.

N—ay, *said Amoranda*, so he is, I own I pity the poor Fellows sometimes, but you know, my Lord, we can't love every-body, they should e'en keep out of Harm's-way.

By this time they were come to the Pond, and the Anglers fell to work, but before they had catch'd any thing to speak of, a Footman came to tell his Lady, Mr. *Pert* was come to wait upon her. Fly, *said Amoranda*, and tell him I come, My Lord, *said she*, you will please to pardon me a moment, I'll go and try if I can engage Mr *Pert* in our Diversion and bring him with me. Without staying for my Lord's Answer, she ran towards the House, and left him with the Angle in his hand: he had now a little time to consider the Lady, but what to make of her he knew not, he took the Letter out of his Pocket, and read it over again, then said to himself, —— 'Twas lost labour in the Lady who wrote it, for *Amoranda* takes no notice of it, her Behaviour is open and free as ever, I shall certainly meet with a critical Minute, and then adieu to Gallantry on this side the Country. Before he had ended his Soliloquies he saw the Lady coming back alone, and went to meet her, What, Madam, *said he*, are you without an Attendant? Yes, my Lord, *said Amoranda*, I could not persuade Mr. *Pert* to venture this Way, he said, the Sun always put out the Stars, and he should give but a glimmering light where there was such a superior Brightness.

Madam,

Madam, *said my Lord*, I once thought Mr. *Pert* so full of himself that he scorn'd Improvement; but I find your Ladyship's Conversation has made a considerable alteration.

Pray, my Lord, have done, *said* Amoranda, for I freely own, I am not proof against Flattery, there is something so inexpressibly pleasing in it —— Lard you Men —— Come, let us catch some Fish, and divert the subject. Hang the Fish, *said my Lord*: Aye *said* Amoranda, for we shall never drown them. But how comes it, my Lord, *said she*, you are so indifferent to such a fine Diversion? Because, Madam, *said he*, I have a finer in view, 'tis to affront the Heart I am so eager in pursuit of, to give way to any other Diversion. Come, Madam, *said he*, let us leave this Drudgery to your Servants, and take a Walk in yonder pleasant Grove, where I may have an Opportunity of laying open to you a Heart ready to burst with Love. Here he took her Hand, and led her towards the Garden, When *Jenny*, *Amoranda*'s Maid, met them, and told my Lord, a Servant was just come to tell his Lordship, his Brother was newly alighted. Never any News was more unwelcome than this to my Lord, who made himself now sure of *Amoranda*'s Consent to any thing he should request of her, and he thought a very few minutes would have compleated his Happiness. He stamp'd, and curs'd his Disappointment, and, with Vexation and Madness in his Looks, took his Leave for that time. He was no sooner gone, than *Jenny* [who was all poor *Amoranda* had now to advise her] began to talk to her Lady about Lord *Lofty*. I am no less concern'd than surpris'd, Madam, *said she*, to see you so free in this Gentleman's Company, after the Account you have had of his Temper in general, and his particular Behaviour to the poor Lady who wrote to you. I wish it were in my Power, *said she*, to prevail with you to see him no more; I read his Designs in his Looks, and am satisfy'd his Intentions are dishonourable. At this *Amoranda* burst out a laughing. The poor Lady that wrote to me, *said she in a jeering Tone*, is one of his Tenent's Daughters, I suppose, whom he, for a Night's Lodging promis'd Marriage, perhaps;

and

and the Creature thinks, because he made a Fool of her, he will and must do so by all the Sex: no, no, *Jenny*, some People, when they are gull'd themselves, would fain make other Folks smart too, but I love to disappoint their Spite, and will, for that reason, take no notice on't.

Madam, said *Jenny*, that Letter looks as if it came from a finer Hand than you seem to think it does, look it over once more, and ———— Aye, said *Amoranda*, *feeling in her Pocket*, but where is it? I had it last Night in the Orange-walk, and have certainly dropt it there, let us go and look for it. No, Madam, said *Jenny*, we need not, if you dropt it there, my Lord has found it, for there he walk'd all the while you were dressing. That can never be, said *Amoranda*, he is a Man of too much Honour to open a Letter directed to me, I am sure, said she, had he found it, I should have had it again, therefore go and look for it. While *Jenny* was gone in quest of the Letter, *Amoranda* began to recollect herself, and remember'd she saw my Lord at a distance putting a Paper into his Pocket, and when she came nearer to him, look'd confus'd; however, she had said so much already in Vindication of his Honour, that she was resolv'd to conceal her own Thoughts; and *Jenny* returning without it, they both went in.

As soon as Dinner was over, *Amoranda*'s Visiters began to flock about her, while she, pleas'd with a Crowd of Admirers, receiv'd them all with equal Complacency, and Singing, Dancing, Musick and Flattery took up her whole Time. Her Heart was like a great Inn, which finds Room for all that come, and she could not but think it very foolish to be beloved by five hundred, and return it only to one; she found herself inclin'd to please them all, and took no small pains to do so; yet had she been brought to the Test, and forc'd to chuse a Husband among them, her particular Inclinations were so very weak, that she would have been at the greatest loss where to fix, tho' her general Favours gave every Man Hopes, because she artfully hid from one what she bestow'd upon another. Among the rest she had two Lovers, who would very fain have brought her to a Conclusion; I shall call one
Froth,

Froth, and the other *Callid*. The latter, tho' he had no cause to despair, grew weary of Expectation, and was resolv'd to have recourse to other Measures. but *Froth* push'd his Fortune forward, and, from an inward Opinion of his own Merit, did not doubt but he should bring *Amoranda* to crown his Wishes, and in a few days bestow herself upon him for Life. One day *Amoranda* and *Froth* were sate in a beautiful Summer-house in the Garden, which had Sashes to the High-way, and here they sate when *Froth* thus accosted her, Madam, *said he*, it is now six Weeks since I first broke my Mind to you; and if I am six more in Suspence it will break my Heart too. I am not insensible of, or unthankful for the Favours you have shewn me; I know I am the happy Man who stands fairest in your Esteem, and since your Eyes declare your Heart is won, why do you retard my Joys? You're a very pretty Fellow, *said* Amoranda *laughing*, to make yourself so sure of a body! how can you believe I shall be so silly, as to think of marrying, while I have so fresh a Bloom upon my Cheeks? No, Mr *Froth*, *said she*, it will be time enough for me to be a Wife, when that dreadful thing Decay gets hold of me; but if it will be any Satisfaction to you, I don't care if I tell you, I have not a less Value for you than for the rest of my Lovers. Madam, *said he*, my Extacy would have been more compleat, had you said a greater. O, *said she*, that's enough for once, but I don't bid you despair. As she spoke these Words, she turn'd her Head, and saw *Callid* coming, and having a mind for a little variety of Courtship, desir'd *Froth* to go and pull a few Nectarines; which he readily did, laughing in his sleeve at poor *Callid*, who he was very sure would meet with a cold Reception. As soon as *Callid* had reach'd *Amoranda*, he began with a very submissive Air, and said, Madam, I am now so far from coming to repeat my presumptive Love, that I come in the highest Despair to resign it, I am too sensible how little I have deserv'd a Return from you, and since my Estate is too small for you —— Your Estate, *said* Amoranda, *interrupting him*, I wonder, Mr *Callid*, you should name it, 'tis trifling indeed compar'd to your Merit. I would have

have you believe I have so good a Taste, as to set the highest Value upon the richest Gem, and I am sorry my Behaviour has given you any despairing Thoughts. Madam, *said he*, I have no cause to complain of your Behaviour, but Hope is a most tiresome thing when it hangs too long upon our Hands; but here comes One to whom I must give place.

Believe me, *said* Amoranda, you mistake, and I will so far comply with your Satisfaction, as to say, you stand as fair in my Esteem as he does. By this time *Froth* came to them, and complaining of Heat threw up the Sash. Some little time after, a Gentleman rid by and threw in a Glove at the Window, *Amoranda*, at whose Foot it fell, took it up, and found there was something in it, which she conceal'd, but was much surpriz'd at the Action. As she was putting it into her Pocket, she saw Lord *Lofty* coming, and leaving *Froth* and *Callid* in the Summer-house went to meet him. What an Age, *said he*, have I been detain'd from my charming *Amoranda*? Oh! come down this Walk, and let me tell you how Absence has tortur'd me ever since I left you.

While my Lord and *Amoranda* were walking in the other part of the Garden, *Froth* and *Callid* began to compare Notes, and talk of the weighty Affair in which they were both concern'd. Mr. *Callid*, said *Froth*, you and I come here upon the same Errand, and in regard to our former Friendship, I must tell you, *Amoranda* is partly dispos'd of, and for that reason I would advise you to desist, a Man's Discretion is greatly to be call'd in question, who, after so many Repulses, as doubtless you have met with, will still go on in a fruitless Attempt. It is true we are both Men of Merit, but Love you know is blind, and if she finds just difference enough to turn the Scale to my Advantage, I think you ought to drop your Amour, and leave the Lady and I to our happy Inclinations. Hum ——— said *Callid*, Yes sure, I must own, a Man of a *Sanguine* Complection, but a little too much upon the Volatile; your Understanding evaporates, and you never had a solid Thought in your Life, otherwise you would tell yourself, this Woman has no more Regard to you than to

all

all Mankind in general perhaps she has given you some Cause to hope, why, she has done the same by me, and is this Minute doing the same by yonder Nobleman, and to-morrow five hundred more shall meet with the same Encouragement, if they attack her No, *Froth*, said he, this way will never do, but if you will give into my Measures, we may find out one that will You and I have been long Friends and old Acquaintance, our Estates are sunk to a low Ebb, though we have hitherto made that a Secret to the World; *Amoranda* is not the Prize we seek after, it is her Fortune we want, and Part of it, at least, we will have, if you will close with my Design Well, said *Froth*, I never sign blank Bonds, let me know what your Design is, and as I like it I will comply with it, but why the Devil, said he, should I lose the Substance for the Shadow? I am sure she bade me not despair, an hour ago, and who would desire more Encouragement?

I find, said *Callid*, you are running away with the old Bait that has catch'd so many Fools already, for my part, I nibbled at it too, but it smell'd so stale I did not like it: and if you will be advis'd by a Friend, who can see as far into a Mill-stone as you can do, you will shun the Trap as well as I. Come then, said *Froth*, let us hear this Scheme of yours. I know, said *Callid*, it will at the first hearing seem a little impracticable, but I don't doubt of convincing you, in a small time, of its Possibility I have often heard *Amoranda* say, she pass'd her whole Evenings in this Summer-house when the Weather is hot, now where would be the Difficulty of whipping her out of this low Window into a Coach provided ready, and carrying her to a House, which I have taken Care of, keeping her with the utmost Privacy till she resolves to marry one of us, and the other shall share the Estate.

Aye, said *Froth*, if this were but as soon done as said, I should like the Contrivance well enough, but pray, said he, don't you think her Maid and she would make a damn'd Noise when they were carry'd off? Yes, said the other, I believe they would, but we might easily prevent it, by a pretty little Gagg for a Minute or two, till we got them into the Coach. Well, said *Froth*,

but

but when we have taken all these Pains, what if she will marry neither of us, and the Hue and Cry catch us, as to be sure it will soon be after us; then, instead of a fine Lady with a fine Estate, we shall each of us get a fine Halter. Thou art a cowardly Puppy, said *Callid*, and I am sorry I have laid myself so open to you; do you think I do my Business by halves? or, that an Affair of such Consequence is to be neglected in any part? No, the Devil himself can't find her where I intend to carry her; and if she will not immediately comply to marry one of us, she will at least come to Terms for her Liberty. you know we cannot stay long in *England*, unless we have a mind to rot in a Jail; and if we can but screw out each of us a Thousand Pounds, we will away to the Czar, and let the Law hang us when it can catch us.

Why, Faith, said *Froth*, I believe such a Project might be brought to bear; but how should we get the Money brought to us? She shall draw a Bill upon her Banker, said *Callid*, for as much as we can get out of her, then we will ride Post to *London* and receive it. And when? said *Froth*, are we to go about this Work? for methinks I would fain have it over; I have still a Fancy *Amoranda* will be mine, and if she be willing to marry me, will you promise not to oppose it? Nay, said *Callid*, if she will marry either of us, I do not see why it may not be me as well as you; I will not make a Deed of Gift of the Lady neither but if it comes to that, she shall e'en draw Cuts for us, and the lucky Loon take her.

What an unhappy Creature is a beautiful young Girl left to her own Management! who is so fond of Adoration, that Reason and Prudence are thrust out to make way for it, till she becomes a Prey to every designing Rascal, and her own ridiculous Qualities are her greatest Enemies! Thus it might have fared with poor *Amoranda*, had not a lucky Hit prevented it, which the Reader shall know by and by. While this Contrivance was carrying on in the Summer-house, my Lord was employ'd in another of a different kind. he thought his Quality sufficient to justify all his Actions, and never fear'd a Conquest wherever he vouchsafed an Attempt.

tempt. Madam, *said he*, why are we to spend our time in this Garden, where so many Interruptions may break in upon our Privacies? I desire an Audience where none but Love may be admitted.

My Lord, said *Amoranda*, did you ever see a finer Goldfinch in your Life than that Cock in the Pear-Tree? That very Cock, my Lord, is Grandsire to all my little warbling Company within doors; I remember him, and know him by a little uncommon Spot over his Eye Oh! it is a charming Bird. I have set a Trap-Cage for him a thousand times, but the dear Creature is so cunning ——— Well, every thing loves Liberty, and so do I; don't you, my Lord? Yes, Madam, *said he*, I lov'd it, and always had it till I knew you, but I am so intangled now in your Charms, I never expect to disengage myself again.

Well, I'll swear, my Lord, said *Amoranda*, that is a pity; methinks a Man of your Gallantry should never marry. Marry! *said my Lord in great Surprize*, no, I hope I shall never have so little Love for any Lady as to marry her. Oons! the very Word has put me into a Sweat, the Marriage-Bed is to Love, what a cold Bed is to Melon-Seed, it starves it to death infallibly. Aye, I believe it does, my Lord, said *Amoranda*, however, one Thing I have often observ'd, when once a Woman is marry'd, no body cares for her but her Husband, and if your Lordship's Remarks be true, not he neither. so that, my Lord, I think we must live single in our own Defence. But, my Lord, *said she*——— what was I going to say——— Oh! pray give me a Pinch of Snuff Nay, Madam, *said my Lord*, this is trifling with my Passion, I cannot live upon such Usage, either ease my Sufferings, or take my Life I'll swear, my Lord, said *Amoranda*, you are a bewitching Man, what a Breach have I made in good Manners by your agreeable Conversation! I left poor Mr. *Froth* and Mr *Callid* in the Summer-house two Hours ago, and had quite forgot they were there. Sure the poor Toads are not there still. Damn the Toads, said Lord *Lofty*, are they a Subject fit for your Thoughts? No, my Lord, *said she*, you see I forgot 'em; but pray let us go in, we shall have the Owls about our Ears, if we stay here any

any longer, it is just dark. Lord *Lofty* was strangely ruffled at this Behaviour; and tho' he still hoped for a pleasing End of his Amour, he plainly saw it would not be so easily attain'd as he at first vainly imagin'd: he therefore took his Leave for that Night, and hoped the next Interview would prove more favourable. *Amoranda* was very glad when she found herself alone, that she might have time to examine the Glove which came so odly into the Summer-house Window. *Jenny*, said she, call for Candles, and come here. When she was sate, and had got Lights, she took out the Glove; Oh! *Jenny*, said she, what a sad Afternoon has my Curiosity had, and how much have I long'd to see what I have got here! She open'd the Top of it, and found a Letter. So, *said she*, here is some new Conquest, but the strangest way of letting me know it that ever was invented. She open'd it, and found these Words;

THIS *Letter, Madam, does not come to tell you I love you, since that would only increase the Surfeit you must have taken with so many hundred Declarations of that kind already; but if I tell you I am in pain for your Conduct, and spend some Hours in pitying your present Condition, it will, I dare say, be entirely new to you, since [though many have the same Opinion of your Behaviour] none have Courage or Honesty enough to tell you so. Consider, Madam, how unhappy that Woman is, who finds herself daily hedg'd in with self-ended Flatterers, who make it their Business to keep up a Vanity in you, which may one day prove your Ruin. Is it possible for any Fop to tell you more than you know already? or, does not your Looking-glass display every one of your fine Features with much more Exactness, than the base, the fawning Rascal, who pretends to dye at your Feet? Spurn him from you, Amoranda, as you would the worst Infection, and believe me rather than him, when I tell you, You are neither Angel nor Goddess, but a Woman, a fine Woman, and there are in this Nation ten Thousand such. If this little Admonition meets with a favourable Reception, you will, upon the first reading of it, discard three Fourths of your daily Attendants, who, like so many Locusts, are striving to devour you.*

Why,

Why, *Jenny*, said *Amoranda*, did you ever hear any thing so impudent in your Life? Oh! Lud! I have not Patience with the familiar Brute, I would give a Thousand Pounds to know the Author; what shall I do to be revenged? Truly Madam, said *Jenny*, I must own, if this be a Conquest, it is made upon a very insulting saucy Lover; and yet I believe he means well too.

Mean well! said *Amoranda*, what good Meaning can he have, who persuades me to banish the Bees, and live in the Hive by myself? No Madam, said *Jenny*, your Ladyship mistakes him, it is the Wasps he would have you discard, who come to sting and steal from those who have a better Title to the Sweets of your Favours: but, Madam, *continued she*, do you think you should know him again, if you see him?

Not I, said *Amoranda*, I never saw his Face, he flung in the Glove before I knew any body was near; and had he not rid away in a Cloud of Dust, I should have thought it had been a Challenge to some of the Gentlemen in the Summer-house, but what vexes me most, *said she*, is his Pity, I always thought a Woman of Youth, Beauty, and such a Fortune as mine is, might raise Envy in many, but Pity in none.

Here the House-keeper came in to speak with her Lady, and put a stop to their present Discourse, by making way for something of greater moment Madam, said she, if your Ladyship be at Leisure, I have a Secret of great Importance to communicate to you. Pr'ythee then, said *Amoranda*, let us have it, perhaps it may put something else out of my Head. Madam, said she, I went this Afternoon into my little Room over the Summer-house, where you know I dry my Winter-Herbs, and while I was turning them, your Ladyship came in with Mr. *Froth*, and *Callid* came to you: you may please to remember, Lord *Lofty* gave you an Opportunity of leaving them, which you had no sooner done, than they began to lay a most dangerous Plot against you,—— [so told her Lady what the Reader has heard already] But, *continued she*, as soon as they had laid their Scheme, Mr. *Callid* said he would go

C and

and provide a Coach, and two or three Villains [like himself] to assist. As soon as he was gone, Mr. *Froth* began to consider with himself what was best to do, stick to the first Design, or discover all to your Ladyship. Now, said he, have I a fair Opportunity of turning *Callid*'s Knavery to my own Advantage, by discovering all to *Amoranda*; so signal a Service can be attended with nothing less than her dear Self, and then I have her without any Hazard or Partner. But then, said he again, as my Friend has well observed, the Devil cannot fix a Woman of her Levity; perhaps, when I have ruined his Design, by telling her the Danger she is in, my Reward may be a Court'sy, and I thank you, Mr. *Froth*, and when it lies in my Power I will serve you again. there is an End of his Hopes, and my own too. No, *said he*, without I were sure of making Sport, I am resolved I will spoil none, and good Luck assist our Undertaking; while yonder Lord is so much at her Service, we need expect no Favours but what we force, so *Callid*, I follow thee to provide for them. Saying thus, he went out of the Garden through the Back-door. Oh! the impudent Rogues! said *Amoranda*. Well, and when, *Brown*, [for that was the House-keeper's Name] is this fine Project to be put in Execution? To-morrow-night, Madam, *said she*. What, said *Amoranda*, whether I am there or no? Though I spend a good deal of Time there, I am not always there. No, Madam, said *Brown*, I forgot to tell your Ladyship that Part of the Contrivance; you are to be entertain'd with a Dance of Shepherds and Shepherdesses in the High-way by Moon-light, just at the Summer-house Window, and if you happen to have any Company, it is to be put off till next Night, under Pretence of one of the Dancers being not well. Very fine, said *Amoranda*, well, since the worthy Gentlemen have begun a Scheme, I will throw in my Counter-Plot among them, and see who will come best off.

Amoranda made her House-keeper a Present of some Guineas, and dismiss'd her. As she went out, a Footman came in and told his Lady, an old Gentleman was just alighted at the Gate, who brought her a Letter, but must deliver it into her own Hand. An old Gen-

Gentleman ! said *Amoranda*; I will wait upon him however. The Stranger enter'd, and gave the young Lady a Letter from her Uncle, in which, when she had open'd it, she found the following Words :

I Have, at last, my dearest *Amoranda* ! *fixed upon such a Person as I think fit to entrust you with, he is one for whom I have the greatest Value, or, to sum up all in one Word, he is my Friend, and as such I desire you will use him, let him in my stead interest himself in all your Affairs. I have so good an Opinion of your Prudence, as to believe you will not often want his Advice, neither will he offer it, unless he finds it necessary: For, though he is an Old Man, he is neither Impertinent, Positive, or Sour. You will, I hope, from my past Behaviour towards you, believe you are very dear to me; and I have no better Way of shewing it for the future, than by putting you into such Hands as* Formator's, *which is the Name of the Bearer; and if you would oblige me, shew it by your Esteem to him, which will confirm me*

Your most Affectionate Uncle,

E. TRAFFICK.

When *Amoranda* had read the Letter, she looked a little earnestly at *Formator*, possibly not very well pleased with a Guardian of such an Age, but she considered she had a Father and Mother to please, in the Person of her Uncle, and he such a One as made up the Loss of both to her: for which reason she resolved to use him, as directed in that Letter, and said to him, with a Smile, I find, Sir, I am no longer my own Mistress, but am now to live under your Restrictions; I promise you, I will always listen to your Advice, and take it as often as I can but I hope, Sir, you will remember I am gay and young, you grave and old, and that the Disparity in our Years may make as great a one in our Tempers: I will therefore make a Bargain with you, if you will bear with a little of my youthful Folly, I will bear with a great deal of your aged Sagacity, and we will be as agreeable to one another, as it is possible for Age and Youth to be.

Madam,

Madam, said *Formator*, I agree to all your Proposals; and shall be very cautious how I presume to advise; and if I ever do so, it shall be when your own Reason must side with me; and I see already you have too much Sense to act against that, unless by Inadvertency. All young People, Madam, are fond of Pleasure, and every Thought that opposes it, is thrust out with Disgrace, but ——— O Lud! said *Amoranda*, I believe you are to be the Chaplain too, if you talk thus much longer, you will argue me out of my Senses; I told you, I could not come into your grave Measures of a sudden. Come, Sir, there is nothing in it, an innocent Chearfulness is much more acceptable both to God and Man, than a crabbed sour Temper, that gives every body the Gripes to look at it. Madam, said *Formator*, you quite mistake me: I am not of that disagreeable Temper you have described, I would have both Young and Old act with that very innocent Freedom you speak of; but what I inveigh against, is an immoderate Love of Pleasure, which generally follows the Young, and too often leads them to Destruction.

Pray, Sir, said *Amoranda*, what is it you call Pleasure?

Madam, said he, I call every thing Pleasure that pleases us; and I dare say, you will own a great many things may, and do please us, which are in themselves very faulty; As for Example, suppose a fine young Lady of a superior Beauty, should spread her *Purlieus* to catch all Mankind, I doubt not but it would give such a One exquisite Pleasure, but it is at the same time a great Fault to give other People exquisite Pain, as the rest of the Sex must certainly feel, when they see one Monopoliser engross the whole Male-World to herself. Nay, said *Amoranda*, there never was any such thing in Nature, as one Woman engrossing the whole contrary Sex; believe me, Sir, ye all love Variety too well for that, and your Affections, like your Money, circulates all the Nation over; so that it is only who can keep their Lovers longest we strive for, not who can keep them always, for that we none of us expect. But come, *Formator*, said she, I must own, you are come at a very critical Juncture, and since my Uncle has

has enjoined me to use you as I would him, after Supper I will give you an early Proof of my Duty to him, and my Confidence in you.

Supper ended, *Amoranda* told *Formator* the whole Story of *Froth* and *Callid*, their base Designs, as well as beggarly Circumstances. *Formator*'s Cheeks glowed with Anger, and in the highest Transport of Rage cried out, How can such a Woman, such a lovely Woman as you are, subject yourself to such Company? Is it possible that fine Sense, which breaks from those lovely Lips with every Word you speak, can find agreeable returns from such Vermin? Can a Man mingle his Wine with Mud, then drink it with Pleasure?

Pardon me, dear Madam, *continued he*, if my Zeal for so good an Uncle to you, and so good a Friend to me, hurries me a little too far, it is not possible for me to see any thing, so deservedly beloved by him, run into the least Weakness; beside, you seem to have too true a Notion of our Sex to be so grosly imposed upon by them. Say no more, good *Formator*, said *Amoranda*, I now promise to be governed in a great measure by you; and since my Uncle has sent you to supply his Place, I will use you with Deference, and bring myself to comply with your Desires as far as possible. This Promise gave the old Gentleman ten thousand Joys, which sate triumphant on his pleased Countenance, and *Amoranda* could not forbear being pleased herself, to see how much he was so. But, Madam, said *Formator*, methinks I long to know how you intend to use those Villains. That, *said she*, you shall do presently. When the Hour is come for the Execution of their intended Project, I design to place two sturdy Footmen, dress'd in mine and *Jenny*'s Cloths, in the Summer-house, the Hour they have appointed, will favour my Design as well as theirs, for ten o'Clock's the Time, and the Moon to be our Light so that they will not easily distinguish betwixt the Fellows and us, till their Sense of Feeling lets them into the Secret, for the Footmen don't want Courage, and I hope my designed Injuries will give them Resentment to it I dare say they will give them love for love, and pay them in their own Coin. What do you think, *Formator*, said she, will not my Contrivance do better than theirs; I hope so, Madam, *said he*, but I have one earnest Request to make to you, and as it is the first, I hope you will not deny me. No, said *Amoranda*, I am sure you will ask nothing I ought to refuse, and therefore I promise. Then, Madam, *said he*, give me leave to personate you in the Summer-House To-morrow Night.

Alas! *said she*, what can your feeble Arm do with such robust Rascals? they will make no more of you than they would of me myself, and methinks I would not have them go off without a good drubbing Fear not, Madam, said *Formator*, this Arm can still do Wonders in so good a Cause, a Vindication of *Amoranda*'s Honour fills my Veins with young Blood, that glows to revenge her Wrongs! Well, said *Amoranda*, I find I have the Remains of a brave Man to take my Part, and since you have so great a Mind to shew your Prowess, pray do; if you happen to be worsted, we will invert the Custom, and instead of your delivering the Distressed Damsel, she shall come and rescue you. This made *Formator* very merry, in spite of all his Gravity: but it was now Bed-time, and he was conducted to his Chamber by the Servants, who were ordered to use him with great Respect The next Morning *Jenny* came to her Lady's Bedside, and told her she had been in the Garden, and had found a Silver Box, I fancy, by the bigness of it, it is Lord *Lofty*'s Snuff Box, said *she*, but there is nothing in it but a Paper. Draw the Curtains, said *Amoranda*, and let me see it, *Jenny* gave her the Box, and when she had opened the Paper, she found it was a Contract betwixt Lord *Lofty* and a Lady, of whom she had often heard, but never saw her; and if Lord *Lofty* receded from his Promise of marrying the Lady, he should then forfeit Ten Thousand Pounds, as an Addition to her Fortune. This Contract nettled *Aromanda* to the very Heart: How *said she*, does my Lord come here to affront me with his Declarations against Marriage, and at the same time is going to engage himself so firmly to another, Base as he is, *said she*, am I a Person fit only to divert those Hours, in which he cannot gain Admittance to one he

likes

likes better? Give me my Clothes *said she*, I will be revenged of him, or lose my Life in the Attempt.

Poor *Jenny*, who never saw her Lady angry in her Life before, began to repent she had said any thing of the Box, and was now afraid her Lady loved Lord *Lofty*. Madam, *said she*, I would not have your Ladyship in such a Passion, for by the Date of this Contract, one would believe my Lord never intended to give it the Lady at all, it has been signed and sealed above a Month, if it was dated at the same time. *Jenny*, said *Amoranda*, recovering herself, and smiling; I fancy by your Looks, you are afraid I have an inward private Inclination for this worthless Peer: but as thou hast always been a faithful honest Servant, I will contribute so far towards thy Ease, as to assure thee, he is upon the same foot with the rest of his Sex, and I know none upon Earth I have a superior Value for, but I own, I have so just a Resentment against his Behaviour to me, that if the Lady this Paper was design'd for will accept of it, I will certainly make her a Present of it to-morrow. But Madam, said *Jenny*, may be, my Lord may come and enquire for it. If he comes to-day, said *Amoranda*, tell him I see no Company, and to-morrow I will put it out of his Reach, —— if my Mind does not alter, *Jenny*, as I believe it will, for upon second Thoughts, it is a Matter of very great Consequence, and I would not contribute to a Man's continual Uneasiness neither, however, I am resolv'd to see no Company to-day, except *Callid* and *Froth*, so pray give Orders accordingly below-stairs.

Jenny was very glad to see her Lady recover her Temper so soon, and when she had obey'd her Commands, she returned to dress her, and then *Amoranda* went down to *Formator*, they paid each other the common Compliment of a Good-morrow, and then went to Breakfast in *Amoranda*'s Closet, for fear of a Visit from Lord *Lofty*, who came before they had well begun. But his Errand was different from what they expected, for he neither enquired for nor had miss'd his Box but when they told him, *Amoranda* saw no Company that Day, I know it, Child, *said he*, she told me yesterday she would see no-body but me; Where is she? then

without

without staying for an Answer, he ran from Room to Room till he found her. *Amoranda* thought his ill-manner'd Freedom proceeded from his Concern for his Box, and was once going to return it, in order to get rid of him, but a better Genius twitched her by the Ear, and bid her keep it. Madam, *said he with his wonted Assurance*, how will you answer this Behaviour to Good-nature? And what have I done to deserve Banishment?

My Lord, said *Amoranda*, I retire sometimes from Company, to make it more acceptable to me when I come into it again, and this, I think, I may do as often as I please, without a Breach in either Good-nature or Good-manners. True, Madam, *said my Lord*, but I would feign be acceptable always. *Amoranda* found by this Answer he had not miss'd his Box, or at least did not suspect she had it, and therefore told him, she was surprized to hear him say he would be always acceptable, after having declared so heartily against Matrimony. I fancy, my Lord, *said she*, you will find a Mistress a little given to Variety, and will hardly like you always as much as you think you deserve. *Formator*, who colour'd at this Discourse, began to take up the Cudgels, My Lord, *said he*, I am sent here by very good Authority, and have a Commission to enquire every Man's Business that comes into this House, I therefore desire to know if, as the Lady says, you declare against Matrimony, what your Designs are in coming here? Pr'ythee Child, said my Lord to *Amoranda*, What queer Old Prig is this? Hark-ye, Friend, said he to *Formator*, your Business now is in the other World, and you would do well to go and prepare for it, without envying us the Pleasures you are past yourself. My Lord, said *Formator*, I am still very capable of Pleasure, and the greatest I can possibly have, is to preserve the lovely Charge committed to my Care, which I will do to the utmost Extremity of my Power, and do here promise you, till you give a better Account of your Intentions, you shall never see her more. *Amoranda* was not very well pleased with what *Formator* said, for tho' she was perfectly insensible of any Passion for my Lord, and knew his dishonourable Designs, she could not think of losing a lover of his Title and Figure without

some

some Emotion: and said to *Formator*, with a little Warmth, I think, Sir, you assume a Power too great for so short a time, and I should take it kindly if you would give me leave to dismiss my Visitors myself This gave my Lord a new Supply of Hope, and he ask'd *Amoranda* Leave to pull him by the Nose. No, my Lord, *said she*, whoever lays a Finger upon him has seen his last of me. Madam, said *Formator*, if I have been so unhappy as to say any thing to disoblige you, I do here in the humblest manner ask your Pardon; but if I am not to take Notice of such Behaviour as Lord *Lofty*'s, I have no Business here, but may forthwith return to him that sent me; for your Part, my Lord, you *dare* not pull me by the Nose. Saying thus he left the Closet, but sent *Jenny* directly up to her Lady, with a Charge to stay with her till my Lord was gone, unless she commanded her otherwise, and then he knew what he had to fear.

Amoranda, on the other hand, found she had vexed *Formator*, which she began to be sorry for, because she knew it would highly disoblige one of the best Uncles in the World, and therefore begg'd my Lord to leave her for that time. He told her he would do ten thousand things to oblige her, and desired but one in return of all. When I understand you, my Lord, *said she*, I shall know what Answer to make; in the mean time, I repeat the Request I have already made you, to leave me now. My Lord with a little too much Freedom snatch'd her to his Arms, took a Kiss, and vanish'd. As soon as he was gone, she went down to *Formator*, and found him in the Parlour, in a very thoughtful melancholy Posture; *Formator*, said she, I am come to tell you, I am under some Concern for what has happened to-day: I have, to oblige you, sent my Lord away, and do here faithfully promise you, I will never come into his Company more without your Approbation. I own, I have the greatest Inclination in the World to please you; and as I believe you sincerely to be my Friend, as such I will always use you, and let this little early Quarrel rivet our future Amity *Formator* was so transported at her good-natur'd Condescension, that he could hardly forbear throwing himself at

her

her Feet; but he considered, Raptures were unsuitable to his Age, so contented himself with saying, Madam, of what Use is our Reason, if we chain it up when we most want it? had yours had its Liberty, it would have shewn you the Villanous Designs of your *Noble* Lover, it would have told you how much he desires your Ruin, that all the love he has for you is to satisfy his own bestial Desires, rob you of your Innocence and Honour, then leave you to the World to finish the Misery he began, by being pity'd and despis'd as long as you live: It is true, Madam, *continued he*, you have a Fortune that sets you above the World, but when I was a young Fellow, we used to value a Lady for Virtue, Modesty, and innate Love to Honour I confess, Madam, *said he*, those are unfashionable Qualities; but they are still the chief Ornaments of your Sex, and ours never think a Woman compleat without them.

Give me leave, Madam, *said he*, to go a little farther, and tell you how great your Misfortunes has been, in being left so long to the Choice of your own Company; your Good-nature, and want of Experience, together with a greedy Desire of Flattery, which [Pardon me, Madam] is a Weakness attending the whole Sex, has encouraged such a heap of Vermin about you, as Providence would not suffer to live, were it not to give us a better Taste for the brave, the just, the honourable and the honest Man

Amoranda was so touch'd with what *Formator* said, that the Tears stood in her Eyes, and she was just going to beg he would have done, when the Bell rung for Dinner, and put a stop to what remained; she was never so lectur'd in her life before; however, she was convinc'd in her own Breast, that every Word was true. As soon as Dinner was over my Friend *Froth* came in, with a Design to sift *Amoranda*'s Inclinations once more, and if he found her leaning to his Side as much as he desir'd, then to discover all, if not, to stay till *Callid* came, and join with him in the Invitation at Night. *Formator*, who was told before he came in who he was, left *Amoranda* and him together, and having a fair Opportunity of trying his Fortune once more he thus began: Madam, I have often look'd with envious Eyes on the

Favours

Favours you confer on Mr. *Callid*; but, Madam, as you cannot have us both, I wish you would [for the Ease of one of us at least] declare in Favour of him you like, and let the other travel. Mr *Froth*, said she, your Friend and you are endowed with such equal Merit, it is hardly possible to say which I like best; beside, if I should declare in Favour of you, Mr. *Callid* would not believe I was in Earnest; and if I should say I like him best, you are too conscious of your own Worth to think I speak from my Heart In short, every thing we do you construe to your own Advantage: if we look easy and pleas'd in your Company we are certainly in Love, if grave and reserv'd 'tis to hide our Love, thus you all imagine we are fond of gaining a Conquest of a Heart, which when we have got it is perhaps so very trifling, that we dispose of it at last as we do of our old Gowns, give it away to our Chamber-maid. But Madam, said *Froth*, if you please, we will lay by general Comparisons, and come to Particulars betwixt *Callid* and myself, and if I from undeniable Reasons prove I deserve best from you, will you promise accordingly to reward me?

I faithfully promise, said *Amoranda*, to reward ye both as ye deserve, but here is Mr *Callid* coming, I'll warrant he has as much to say for himself as you have [Mr. *Callid* came to 'em, and said to *Amoranda*] I have provided a little Country Entertainment for you Madam if you will do me the Honour to see it anon. You are always so very obliging, said *Amoranda*, — but you know, Mr. *Callid*, I never go far from home. No farther than your own Summer-house, Madam, *said he*, I have engag'd a few of my Tenants to appear in a Rural Dress, and give you a Shepherd's-Dance; they have been practising this Fortnight, and I am in hopes they may prove perfect enough to give you some Diversion, I have ordered them to be there exactly at Ten o'Clock, by which Time the Road will be quiet, and the Moon up: And Madam, said *Froth*, a Dance of Shepherds and Shepherdesses looks so *natural* by Moon-light ——Yes, said *Amoranda*, so it does; and I promise myself already a great deal of Pleasure from the Hour ye speak of: but I wish I had known in the morning, I would have

engaged

engaged Lord *Lofty* to come himself, and have brought some Ladies with him. No matter, *said she*, we will have it to ourselves: And Gentlemen, I desire ye will not sup before ye come; for I shall take care of a small Repast for ye, and we will sup in the Summer-House that we may be near our Diversion Come then *Froth*, said *Callid*, we will go and see them do it once more before they perform in the Lady's view; for nothing could be so great a Baulk to me, as to have any thing wrong where she is to be a Spectator. As soon as they were gone, *Amoranda* called *Formator*, and bid him chuse a Companion for the Exploit in Hand, for she had promised the two Gentlemen a Supper in the Summer-House, and she would feign have them have a Bellyfull.

Formator took the young Lady's Advice, and went to chuse a good sturdy Fellow, to personate *Jenny*, while he did as much by *Amoranda*; and when the appointed Time was come, they took their Places in the Summer-house, with each a good Crab-tree-Cudgel by him: and after a little Expectation, the two impudent Varlets came, ask'd for *Amoranda* with their wonted Sauciness; and being told she was in the Garden, flew to their hop'd-for Prize. *Callid* ran as he thought to *Amoranda*, and catching her in his Arms, cried, No Resistance, Madam, by *Jove* you must along with me; *Froth* did the same by the supposed *Jenny*; and just as they were going to gag them, and call their Associates, who waited in the Lane for the Sign, to their Assistance, the two Ladies began to handle their Cudgels, and laid about them with such Dexterity, that the Ravishers were almost knock'd o' the Head before they could believe they were beaten, so great was their Surprize, and so little did they expect to meet with such Resistance: but when they found the Blows came faster on, without regard to either Sex or Quality, they began to draw their Swords, *Formator* struck *Callid*'s out of his Hand, and the Footman tripp'd up *Froth*'s Heels, before he could get his out of the Scabbard; which he would not have attempted to do, but that he thought his Antagonist a Woman. All this while the two Ladies laid on so unmercifully, that they began to cry

Quarter

Quarter and beg for Mercy, when the Noise reached the House, and they saw *Amoranda*, with Lights before her, coming in a great Surprize, to see what the Matter was. *Callid*, when he saw her and *Jenny*, could hardly believe his half-beaten-out Eyes, but stood stareing, first at the real Lady, and then at the feign'd one; but when he found how Matters went, he cry'd *Froth*, thou Villain, thou hast betray'd me. If I have, said *Froth*, I am ill rewarded for it, and believe I shall never stir either Hand or Foot again. Well Gentlemen, said *Amoranda*, are the Shepherds come? when does the Dance begin? It is over, Madam, said *Formator*, these Gentlemen have been cutting Capers this half Hour to a sorrowful new Tune. Why, what is the matter? said she, I hope you have not hurt them.

Nothing Madam [said *Formator*] but *Harry* and I took a Frolick to sit here this Evening in Masquerade, and these two Beaus had a mind to ravish us, I think, for they were going to gag us. I am sorry Sir [said he to *Callid*] that I was forced to exercise my Cudgel upon you, I hope you will excuse it, had I been in another Dress I would have used another Weapon. I think [said *Amoranda*] he did not stand upon so much Ceremony with *you*, for I see he has drawn his Sword, though he took you for a Woman. Yes [said *Callid*] ready to choak with Rage, Despair and Disappointment, I took him for you, on whom I would have had a glorious Revenge had it prov'd so. Oh! Death and Fury [said he] what malicious Devil interpos'd? but it is some Satisfaction to tell you how I would have used you, had Fortune been so kind as to have put you in my Power; know then, proud Beauty, I would—— I know already [said *Amoranda* interrupting him] as much of your Designs as ye can tell me but Gentlemen [said she] if the *Czar* should not take ye into his Service when ye have received the Money from my Banker, pray let me know, and I will make a better Provision for you. I have an Uncle going to the *Indies* who wants Slaves; and I believe, at my Request he would take ye into his Service: in the mean time, do me the Favour to leave this Place, for I have ha' as much of your Company as I can dispense.

D

hope Madam [said *Froth*, whose Tongue was the only Part about him he could stir without Pain] you have more Hospitality in you, than to turn us out of your House in this Condition; you had more need send for a Surgeon to set our dislocated Joints in Order, and wrap us up in Sear-Cloth: I don't believe I shall live a Week. That [said *Amoranda*] would be a great Pity, the World would have a sad loss of so worthy a Man, but I hear ye have a Coach hard by, I shall order two of my Servants to load each of them with a Knave, and convey ye both to it I hope ye will own I have been as good as my Word; I promised ye a Supper and Desert, and I believe ye have had both. Upon which she and her Retinue went away, leaving the two batter'd Beaus in the Summer-house, till a Couple of lusty Fellows came to take them up and shoot the Rubbish into the Coach. The Servants who carried them away, left them and returned home, and as soon as they were gone *Callid* accused *Froth* of Treachery, and laid the whole Discovery to his Charge. *Froth* declared his Innocence, and urged his own Share of the Suffering as a Proof he was so. but *Callid*'s Disappointment had soured his Temper, as well as made him desperate, and he was resolved to be deaf to all *Froth* could say in his own Vindication. and though they were both so bruised they could hardly stand, he made the other draw, who was innocent in Fact, tho' not in Intention. and though they lived like Scoundrels they went off like Gentlemen, and the first Pass they made took away each other's Life.

This News soon reached *Amoranda*'s Ear, whose tender Heart felt a great deal of Pity for the tragical Catastrophe But *Formator* told her, he thought she ought rather to rejoice, if she had a true Sense of a Fellow Creature's Sufferings, for [said he] when once a Man has outlived his Fortune and his Friends, his next Relief is the Grave. He had now pretty well cleared the House of the Catterpillers that infested it, and began to take the greatest Delight in his Charge his constant Care was to divert her from all the Follies of Life, and as she had a Soul capable of Improvement, and a flexible good Temper to be dealt with,

he

made no doubt but one day he should see her the most Accomplish'd of her Sex: in Order to which, he provided a choice Collection of Books for her, spent most of his Time with her, diverted her with a Thousand pleasant Stories, possibly of his own making; and every Moment was lost to *Formator* that was not spent with *Amoranda*.

Lord *Lofty* had made two Visits during this Time, but *Formator* would not admit him, and by *Amoranda*'s Consent told him she was engaged: which nettled the Peer so much, that he writ to her in the Bitterness of his Soul the following Words;

MADAM,

IF *it were possible for me to unriddle a Woman's Behaviour, I should immediately try my Skill upon yours; but as I believe Men of deeper Penetration than I have been baffled, I must even [with the rest] leave you to your own wild Mazes: One Day caress'd, the next cashier'd, a third receiv'd again, and a fourth quite banish'd. However, though this be a common Treatment from most of your Sex, I never had Cause to mind it so much in you, till this old whimsical Fellow came to give you ridiculous Advice, and your Adorers endless Torment. What the Devil have our Years to do with this? Or why must his pernicious Counsel disturb our Pleasures? If you have that Value for me still, which you once gave me Reason to hope you had, you will meet me in the little Grove at the End of your own Garden about Nine o'Clock, where I will acquaint you with some Secrets you never knew before. I have contriv'd a Way to it without coming near the House, and your Old Argus will never suspect you, if you come alone to the Arms of*

Your Faithful Admirer,

LOFTY.

Before *Amoranda* had done reading this Letter, a Servant came and told her, a Gentleman on Horseback at the Gate desired to know if he might be admitted to her Presence for a quarter of an Hour; his Business was a little urgent, but it would be soon over.

Poor *Amoranda* had been so lately in Jeopardy, that she was now afraid of every-body, and durst do nothing without *Formator*, who went to know the Gentleman's Name, but when he came to the Gate, he saw a poor, thin, pale, meagre young Creature, hardly able to sit his Horse, who look'd as if he wanted a Doctor more than a Mistress. When he had view'd him well, he was asham'd to ask him any Questions, thinking he might as well be afraid of a Shadow as such a Skeleton as he was; and therefore desired him to alight, which with the Help of two Servants he had with him he did. *Formator* conducted him in, and left him with *Amoranda*, when the Stranger was sate [for he was very ill able to stand] he first begg'd *Amoranda* to shut the Door, that none might be Witness to his wretched Tale but herself, and then with a flood of Tears begun thus:

It is the Way of the Damn'd, Madam, to desire all Mankind should be in their own miserable State, but though I am as wretched as they, I am not so envious: And it is to prevent your Fate, and receive your Pity, that I am come at this time to you. Sir, said *Amoranda*, your Looks without your Tale call for Pity, and I intreat you to drink a Glass of somethink to comfort you, before you spend the few remaining Spirits you have left, in a Story which I foresee will give you Pain in the repeating. Alas! Madam, said he, Food and I are become Strangers to each other, but it is all the Pleasure I have to repeat my Wrongs, and my tortured Heart is never capable of a Moment's Ease but when I am complaining. *Amoranda* was in the utmost Perplexity to find out what Whining Romantick Lover she had got, and could not imagine where the Adventure would end, or how her Fate came to be concerned in the Matter. But the poor Afflicted soon let her into the Secret, which she begun to be impatient to know. Madam, said the Stranger, I am now going to tell you a Story which will melt you into the greatest Pity: but before I proceed, intreat you will not be too severe upon my Conduct, or say when I have done, I have reaped the Desert of my own Folly. *Amoranda* promised her best Attention without any Reflection at all; and the Stranger thus begun.

The first Thing I am to inform you of, Madam, is my Sex, which is not what it appears to be. I am a Woman, a wretched, miserable, unhappy Woman! My Father was the eldest Son of an Ancient Family, born to a very plentiful Estate, and when he died left only one Son and myself. My Mother died soon after I was born, and my Father left me wholly to the Care of my Brother, who was at Age when he died; and my Fortune which was Five Thousand Pounds, was to be paid me when I married, or was of Age, and to be kept in my Brother's Hands till then. I was then about fourteen Years old, and my Brother who was Father too, used me with all the Tenderness that could be expected from so near a Relation, and had he kept within the Bounds of Honour, and loved me only as a Sister, I might have reckoned myself in the Number of the Happy. A whole Year passed over with the greatest Innocence, and my Brother's Love seemed faultless and natural; but when I was turned of Fifteen, in the Height of my Bloom and Pride of Beauty, I was one day dressed to most Advantage for a Ball in the Neighbourhood, when my Brother came in, and looking stedfastly at me, *Altemira!* said he, O *Altemira!* you are too lovely. Then snatching me to his Bosom, pressed me with a Warmth which a little surprized me. I broke loose from his Embraces and ask'd him what he meant, he seem'd a little confounded, and left the Room. I confess I was under some Apprehension of an approaching Misfortune, but was loth to harbour any Thought to the Disadvantage of so dear a Brother, and therefore imputed the Action rather to Chance than Design. He came to the Ball, but would neither dance nor speak, nay, nor so much as look at any thing but me, which only I took Notice of. When the Company broke up, he convey'd me home, and as we were going he sigh'd, and said, I had made him very wretched. How! Brother! [said I, not willing to understand him] by what Behaviour am I so wretched to make you so? Oh! *Altemira!* said he, cease to talk, your Actions had been better had they been worse, for who can see so much Perfection without Love, without Adoration? Oh! *Altemira!* I must, I will enjoy you. It is not possible

for

for me to tell you, Madam, how shocking this was to me, I could hardly keep from swooning in the Coach, but my Passion found vent at my Eyes. And with Ten Thousand Tears I begg'd him to recal his scattered Senses, to arm his Reson for his own Defence, to consider I was a Sister; nay, a Sister who was left wholly to his Care, and one who had none to fly to for Redress of Injuries but him. And am I so entirely miserable, as to find my Ruin where I seek my Sanctuary? said I. Oh! by the Ashes of our dead Father and Mother, by all the Ties of natural Affection, of Honour, Virtue, and every thing we hold dear in this Life, if you have any Regard to my Welfare or your own, stifle this guilty Flame, and let me quench it with my Tears.

I wish *Altemira*, said he, I could quench it with my own, but it is grown too fierce to be extinguished; I have kept it under a great while, and with my utmost Care endeavoured to suppress it. but alas! my Attempts were in vain, it was too powerful for me, and is now broken out with such Violence, that unless you stop its Force, I must consume to Ashes in the midst on't. My Heart at those Words sunk both with Horror and Pity, I saw an only Brother, whom I dearly and tenderly loved, a black Criminal, entangled in a guilty lawless Love, while I, who only had the Power of relieving him, lay under an indispensable Duty of refusing to do so. As soon as we alighted out of the Coach we went to our different Apartments, how my poor Brother spent his Night I know not, but mine went on with a heavy Pace; I counted every dull Hour as it came, and bathed in Tears lay thinking how to extricate myself from the miserable Condition I was in. I found my unfortunate Brother was too far gone to be brought to Reason, and had often heard, a desperate Disease must have a desperate Cure: I therefore resolved to end his Ruin, by Absence, and go where he should never see me, till I was satisfied he had got the better of his own Folly.

In Order to this, I got up when the Clock struck Four, and calling my Maid, who lay in a Closet just by me, I made her pack up some Clothes for me and herself; and taking all my Mother's Jewels, which

were

were now mine, and what ready Money I had, we went down unheard or obferved by any body, and took the Road to a Wood hard by: I well knew as foon as my Brother was up, he would as ufual come to enquire after my Health, and when he mifs'd me, make ftrict Enquiry after me; I therefore thought it moft advifable to ftay a Day or two where we were, till the Search was a little over, and then purfue my intended Journey. My Maid favour'd my Defign, though fhe knew it not, by ftepping into the Buttery before fhe came out, and filling her Pocket with fomething for her Breakfaft, which we lived upon two Days. In a Thicket in the Wood we found a Shepherd's Hut deferted by the Owner, where we lay that Night; and the next Day towards Evening we ventured to a Farmer's Houfe, where for a Guinea to the Man, who was newly come, and knew neither of us, he undertook to carry us both where I directed him. When I was about Eleven Years of Age, we had a Female Servant who was Cook, and had lived in the Family many Years. She juft then married away, and to her I went: fhe was exceedingly furpris'd to fee me at fuch an early Hour [for we rid all Night] and no better attended. Here [faid I to the Man that brought us] there is your Hire, and a Crown to drink, make the beft of your way home again. I now thought my felf the happieft Creature upon Earth, for I faw my felf fafe, and had One to whom I durft intruft my Secret, which I never did to my Maid *Kitty*, becaufe I would not expofe my Brother, and for which fhe ow'd me, and paid me a Grudge. The Woman to whofe Houfe we were come, was always called when fhe lived with my Father by the Name of her Place, *Cook*, and fo I fhall call her for the future. She married a Gardiner, who liv'd for fome time with Lord *Lofty*. I prefume, Madam, faid fhe, you know the Man, and fo do I too well. It was, no doubt, decreed, that I fhould never have Reft, otherwife I fhould have mifs'd his fatal Acquaintance. Pity, Madam, faid *Amoranda*, give me leave to interrupt you fo long, as while I ask you, Whether you ever favour'd me with a Letter in your life? That, Madam, faid *Altemira*, you fhall know prefently. I had

not

not been three Days at *Cook*'s before my Lord came that way a-hunting, and just at Dinner-time, being very hungry, he popp'd in upon us before we were aware of him. It is possible you will not readily believe I ever had a Face worth looking at, while you see no Remains of a good one, but —————— There I interrupt you again said *Amoranda*, for though you have now a livid, pale Complection, your Features are still fine, and a little Quiet of Mind would raise those fallen Cheeks to their usual Plumpness. Be that as it will, said *Altemira*, Lord *Lofty*, saw something in it which he thought worth his Notice, and he no sooner cast an Eye upon me than he vow'd an everlasting Love. He took *Cook* aside, and found out who I was, but not the Occasion which brought me there. He spent the remaining part of the Day with us, and most of the Night, before he could be persuaded to leave us, and next Day he came again, and said Ten Thousand Things to win a foolish Heart. And I must own, I began to be too well pleased with every Word that fell from his bewitching Tongue, he soon perceiv'd it, and as soon took the Advantage of my Weakness. One Day as we were alone he begun to take some Liberty, which I was not very well pleas'd with, and said, My Lord, you abuse the Freedom I have given you, I have hitherto believ'd your Intentions Honourable. You know best whether they are so or no, if they are not, be assured your Quality will stand for very little in my Esteem. And till I am better satisfied in that Point, your Lordship will excuse me if I see you no more. Saying thus I left the Room, and went to my own, where I lock'd myself up, and came no more out while my Lord stay'd, which was some Hours. The next Morning, before my Eyes were well open'd to read it, a Letter came from him fill'd with Ten Thousand Protestations of his Sincerity, and if I would but give him Leave once more to throw himself at my Feet, he would soon convince me of his Reality. I have already own'd, his oily Tongue had made an Impression on my Heart; and I took a secret Pleasure in hoping all he said was true. I sent no Answer back by the Messenger, which was giving a tacit Consent to another Interview, and I
saw

saw him at my Feet before I thought the Meſſenger could have returned. Oh! what an aſſiduous Creature is Man before Enjoyment! and what a careleſs negligent Wretch after it! Dear *Altemira*, ſaid my Lord, Why do you uſe me with ſuch Contempt? What ſhall I do to convince you of the real Value I have for you? Is there one Oath left I have not ſworn to confirm my Love to you? Or can my Actions diſplay themſelves with greater Ardency than I have already ſhewn? Yes, my Lord, ſaid I, there is one Action yet remains which muſt authorize all the reſt, that once done I am yours for ever, but till then you know what you have to truſt to. I underſtand you, Madam, ſaid the baſe Deceiver, and I greatly approve your cautious Proceedings. You ſhall ſoon be ſatisfy'd in every Point, and I will break through all my own Meaſures to make you eaſy; To-morrow's Sun ſhall ſee us one. After this Promiſe he ſtaid not long, but left me in the greateſt, the higheſt Tranquillity I ever knew. When my Lord was gone, *Cook* came to me, and told me, ſhe was afraid there was ſome Juggle betwixt my Lord and *Kitty*; for I have ſeen him whiſpering with her twice, ſaid ſhe, and beg you will have a Care what you do, and how you truſt her; ſhe is very ſullen at ſomething, and has been out of Humour ever ſince ſhe came here.

I know it, ſaid I, and the Reaſon is, becauſe I have not let her into the Secret of leaving my Brother's Houſe. I wiſh, ſaid *Cook*, you would part with her, I do not like her, I can recommend one to you juſt now, who will, I am ſure, be very juſt to you.

No, ſaid I, I will firſt be convinc'd of her Behaviour, I hate a ſtrange Face. Well, Madam, ſaid *Cook*, I wiſh you may not repent it. For my part, I was ſo full of Satisfaction at the Promiſe my Lord had made me, that I could find Room for no other Thought, and went to Bed two Hours ſooner than uſual, that I might indulge it without Interruption. As ſoon as Day appear'd my poor unwary Heart gave a freſh Alarm to Love and Joy; and when I heard the Family ſtirring, I got up and dreſſed me to the beſt Advantage, expecting every Hour to ſee my Lord attended by his Chaplain, at laſt I ſaw my Lord enter, but no Chaplain,

lain: he came to me and said, My *Altemira*, I am now come to remove all your Doubts; take this [said he, pulling out a Paper] and let it convince you how much I love. I opened the Paper, and found it a Promise to marry me, with a Bond of Ten Thousand Pounds, if ever he receded from his Word. I own I was much pleased with the Paper, which he gave me in great Form, as his Act and Deed, before *Cook* and her Husband, who were both Witnesses to it: But I could not find out the Meaning of it, and said, my Lord, if you design to marry me, what Occasion is there for all this Formality and Stuff? I presume you are your own Master; what then retards your Design? I will tell you, my dearest *Altemira*, said he, when you and I are alone. Well, said I, let me go and lay by this Paper, and I'll wait upon you again. I went up to my Chamber, and lock'd it up in a Scrutore which stood in the Room, and of which I had the Key, and then return'd to my Lord, whom I found all alone. Well, my Lord [said I, with a much freer Air than usual] now we are alone, pray let me hear this Secret.

Altemira [said this base Impostor] I now look upon you with a Husband's Eyes, you are *in foro Conscientiæ* my Wife, and as such I will entrust you with all I know. About nine Months ago, I saw a Lady whom I admired then, as I do you now, and after I had made my Addresses to her some time, she consented to crown my Wishes, and we were to be married in a Month's time, but before it was expir'd [with the true Spirit of Inconstancy which reigns in most of your Sex] she jilted me, and admitted another, to whom she is to be married next Week. Now, my Dear, said he, should I marry first, she will fling all her own Levity at my Door, and say the Falshood was mine, for which Reason, since she is so near Marriage, I will deny myself the Pleasure of thy dear Arms a few Days, rather than undergo the Scandal of doing an ill Action to a fine Woman. Here was a Gloss set upon as base a Design as ever Villain invented, and I, who look'd upon all he said as from an Oracle, gave a pleasing Ear to it. He staid not late that Night, but came again early next Day, for he liv'd within three little Miles of *Cook*'s House,

and

and every time he came grew more familiar with me; I must confess to you, good Madam, I loved this Ingrate to Distraction, and after such a firm substantial Proof of his, as I had lock'd up, I thought myself exceedingly secure. My Fear and Caution which used to attend me constantly now left me, and I had no other Desires than to please my Undoer. Three or four Days after he had given me the above-mentioned Paper, he came and said, My *Altemira*, you have never seen my House, I desire you will go with me to-day, and dine there, I hope I have given you too many Demonstrations of Love, to leave you any Room for Fear. My Lord, said I, it is now my Interest to believe every thing that is good of you, and I have no Fear of any thing but want of Power to please you always. After some other Discourse I went up to dress, and you may be sure I left no Charm behind me, which I could possibly take with me. *Cook* was not willing I should go, but durst not be known to persuade me from it, because my Lord was a good Friend to her Husband; however I ventur'd to go, and met with all the civil Treatment in the World. I now thought myself at home, and was pleased to think how soon I should give my Brother an Account of my good Fortune from thence: but alas! my Doom was near, my eternal Destruction just at hand. When we were at Dinner a Letter came for my Lord, which he read, and gave it to me; it was an Account of the Lady being married, whom he had some Days before told me of. Now, *Altemira*, said he, it is our Turn, To-morrow you and I will join our Hands. When Dinner was over he sent his Chaplain for a Licence, who accordingly brought one, which he shewed me. The Afternoon we spent in different Diversions; and at Night, when I would have gone to *Cook*'s, my Lord said I should never leave the House till it was my own, and begg'd I would be satisfy'd to stay all Night. He told me I should have a Room to myself and Maid, and in the Morning *Hymen* should crown our Wishes. I own I was not long persuading to comply, but soon consented to my own undoing: for about One o'Clock, when all the House was gone to Bed, I heard a little
knock-

knocking at my Chamber-door, *Kitty* immediately rose, without saying any thing to me, and opened the Door; my Lord enter'd, and came to my Bedside. *Kitty*, the Treacherous *Kitty*, put on her Clothes and left the Room, as she had been instructed. My dearest *Altemira* said my Lord, it is impossible for me to rest while you are so near me; give me a Bridegroom's Privilege, and let me lie down by you. I found myself under some Concern at his Proposal, but consider'd, a few Hours would give him a just Title to all I had in Possession: I called every Circumstance to my Memory; the firm Engagement I had under his Hand, the Letter from *London* of the Lady's Marriage; the Licence, and Preparations which were made, and the Millions of Oaths and Vows which I had receiv'd from a perjur'd Tongue, of an eternal Love; all these, in Conjunction with an unguarded Hour, made me a Prey to the basest of Men. In short, Madam, he gained his Ends; and after some Hours Enjoyment got up, and left me. *Kitty*, when he went out, came in again, but I was so little apprehensive of my own Fate, that I said not much to her, but got up and reassum'd all my Charms. When we were at Breakfast, my Lord said with a sort of Raillery, It shall never be said, Madam, that you come to me to be married, if you think fit, we'll confirm our Vows at *Cook*'s, as you call her. With all my Heart, my Lord, said I, she is Witness to our Contract, let her also see our Nuptials. When we had done the Coach was order'd to the Door, and Lord *Lofty* put me into it, and accompanied me to *Cook*'s, Now, Madam, said he, I will leave you for an Hour, and then return with my Chaplain: In the mean time, said he to *Cook*, send for what Provisions you think fit for Dinner to my House, and do you dress it well, and I will help to eat it. This was no sooner said, than my Lord whipt into the Coach and drove away. As soon as he was gone my Maid came to me and said, Madam, I have heard by Chance my Mother is not well; I beg you will give me Leave to go and see her. If she recovers I will return, if not, you may be pleased to provide yourself of another, I shall give you an early Account. *Kitty*, said I, it falls out unluckily

for

for you; but who can help Misfortune? I am not willing to part with you, and if you can return in a Month's time, so long I will stay for you. The Jade thank'd me, and went away.

I was now left alone with honest *Cook*, then she asked me, if I was married? I told her No, but very near it. She shaked her Head, and said, she hoped I had brought the same Treasure back with me which I took to my Lord's, for he was going this Morning to *London*. How do you know [said I in a distracted Tone] I went, said she, to enquire for you last Night, when I found you came not back, but was not admitted to see you, and I then heard Orders given, for the best Horses to be gotten ready for *London* in the Morning. Good Heaven! said I, can this be true? Is there no such Thing as Justice in Man? No Faith in their Oaths and Vows? Oh *Cook*! said I, if you are still my Friend, as I hope you are, send thither this Minute to know the Truth of what you tell me. But I fear, continued I, there is too much in it, both by his bringing me here again, and by *Kitty's* going away, that Wench has certainly sold me to him, and I am undone; for Oh! said I, all is gone. While *Cook* was preparing to send to my Lord's, a Footman came with a Letter for me; he just deliver'd it, and went off, which I open'd and read, as follows.

MADAM,

AN Unlucky Accident has forced me away to London; *it is so very sudden, that I have not Time to excuse my going. I hope, at my Return, I shall find you where I left you, and you shall find me,*

Your most Obedient,

LOFTY

As soon as I had read this Letter my Spirits sunk, and I remained breathless in my Chair; when *Cook* came in to know what News, she saw the Paper dropt at my Foot, and guessed something of the Contents. I was conveyed to my Bed, where I lay for some Days in a most miserable Condition; though in the midst of all my cruel Reflections, I found my Conscience clear'd myself, and I was in Hopes my Lord's Bond would, in some measure, justify my Actions to the World. With this little Satisfaction I got up, and went to the Scrutore, to take out and look at all the Hopes I had left; I fully design'd, if he refused to marry me at his Return, to sue his Bond, recover the Ten Thousand Pounds, and chuse a quiet Retirement from the World, where I might end my Days in Peace: but Oh! what Tongue can tell my Surprise, Confusion and Despair, when I miss'd the Paper, which I had put into a Silver Box, and both were gone together.

I called *Cook* with a feeble Voice, who came to me, to hear my new Complaints. O *Cook*! said I, my Misery is now compleat, I have lost my Lord's Bond and Promise of Marriage; it was in a Silver Box in this Scrutore. A Silver Box! said *Cook*, I saw *Kitty* put one in her Pocket the fatal Day you went to my Lord's, and ask'd her what was in it? she said, her Lady's Patches: You must trust that wicked Quean, said she, whom I always disliked, and now —— Aye, said I, and now she has undone me for ever, may her Perfidy to me meet with a just Reward. Nature was so far spent in me by my previous Trouble, that I sunk under this new Addition, past all Hope of ever rising more, I was some Weeks before I had the use of my Reason, but lay like a stupid Log, taking what Sustenance they gave me, because I knew not what I did. At last, by degrees I recovered my Senses, but was infinitely less happy than when I had none, because I was then free from Reflection, my cruel Disquiet of Mind made so great an Alteration in my Face, that when I came to look at it, I could not believe I was *Altemira*. After I had been in this Condition four Months, I heard Lord

Lofty was return'd from *London*; I immediately writ to him in the most supplicating Terms, but he would not vouchsafe me an Answer. I writ again, and he sent it back unopen'd. I had once a mind to go to him, but I thought his Behaviour to myself would be of a piece with that of my Letters, and I should only expose myself to his Servants, and pick up new Matter for fresh Grief. but I soon found why I was used with so much Contempt, and heard he made his Addresses to the Rich, Young, Beauteous *Amoranda*. I own Madam, your Person and Fortune have an infinite Advantage over mine; but a Man, who is resolv'd to be a Libertine, has no true Value for a Woman's good Qualities; the best she can shew to please him, is to give into all his Brutal Pleasures: And as I was sure you would shun such a Lover, I own, I did write a Line to let you into the Temper of the Man. But now Madam, since I have told you my Wrongs, I hope I have engaged your Justice, Goodness and Pity; and you will no longer encourage his Addresses, but look upon them with the same Contempt as from a married Man. Madam, said *Amoranda*, your Case I own is very deplorable, and what would give me a sensible Affliction, were it not in my Power to do you some Service; but I believe I can make you a very acceptable Present, and will contrive a Way of serving you beside. At those Words *Amoranda* left *Altemira*, and returned with the Box and Bond; This, Madam, said she, is, I presume, the Loss you have so much lamented, and I do assure you, Lord *Lofty* has not been at *London* since his Injuries to you, but at a Seat he has just by this House, and there he is now. That Box I have now given you, he accidentally dropt in my Garden, nor does he know I have it, and till I see you as firmly his, as he has promised you should be, I will never leave contriving.

The Sight of Lord *Lofty*'s Bond gave poor *Altemira* a Satisfaction not to be expressed, the Blood which had so long forsaken her Cheeks, began to run again in its wonted Channels, and Joy diffused itself in every Feature of her Face: Is it possible, said she, that I am so happy as to recover this Testimony of his Villany! It is some little Satisfaction for my lost Honour, that I have this small Justification of myself. It is a very great one to me, said *Amoranda*, that I can contribute towards it; and if I can but gain one Point I have in my Head, I hope I shall see you perfectly easy; but I have an Old Gentleman in the House, who must be let into the Secret, or nothing can be done.

Madam, said *Altemira*, my Secrets are too well known to the World; engage who you will in the Secret, but spare me the Confusion of hearing it. Then, said *Amoranda*, I will leave you employed while I go to my Guardian, and desire you will write a Letter to Lord *Lofty*, to let him know you have recovered the Bond and Contract, which your perfidious Servant return'd to him, and that you expect all the Satisfaction the Law can give you; then leave the rest to me. Here she left *Altemira*, and sent *Jenny* with Pen and Ink to her, while she told *Formator* the whole Story; he needed no Addition to Lord *Lofty*'s Character, to confirm him it was a very bad one; however, his Indignation was ready to boil over, and he expressed himself, as every Man of Honour would do upon such an Occasion. *Formator*, said *Amoranda*, I have this poor Creature's Wrongs so much at Heart, that I shall never rest till I recover her Quiet; but you must give me Leave, because I have promised never to see Lord *Lofty* more, unless I have your Consent for it, and without seeing him nothing can be done.

Madam, said *Formator*, I applaud your just and generous Design, and am so far from desiring to hinder it, that I will be your Assistant to the utmost of my Power. Then, said *Amoranda*, give me leave to send for my Lord this Minute, and do you abscond. *Formator* consented to her Proposal, and she writ the following Lines to my Lord, and sent them by a Footman just then.

My Lord,

I *Do not want Inclination to meet you where you desired at Nine; but my* Argus, *as you have some time called him,*

him, is gone abroad for this Night, so that we may have an Interview within doors. You know the Hand so well, that this Paper needs no other Subscription, but that I am Yours.

As soon as she had dispatched this Letter, she went to see how *Altemira* went on with hers, and found she had just finish'd it. I am beforehand with you, said *Amoranda*, for I have writ to my Lord since I saw you, and sent it. It is an Invitation to a Man I now hate, and if I can but gain my Ends upon him——— Come, let me see what you have writ. She took the Letter from her trembling Hand, and read;

IF Prayers and Tears could mollify an Unrelenting Obdurate Heart, yours had long ago been softened into Justice and Pity, but as they have failed me so often, I think it needless to try them any more. To tell you, my Lord, of Heaven and Conscience, would only serve to make you Sport; but methinks, you should have some little Regard to your bleeding Honour, which lies stabb'd and mangled in a Thousand Places by your own Barbarities.

However, my Lord, I am now to tell you, a Fortunate Hit has put you into my Power, and the Contract you gave me, and corrupted my Servant to steal from me, is once more fall'n into my Hands. I dare say, you will easily believe I intend to carry it as far as the Law will bear, but am still forced to wish you would do a Voluntary piece of Justice to

Your Injured

ALTEMIRA.

This Letter was sealed, and directed for Lord *Lofty*, and the Summons *Amoranda* had sent him, soon brought him to receive her Commands. In the mean time, neither *Altemira* nor *Formator* knew any thing of her Design, but as she hoped it would be attended with good Success, she was resolved to have the Merit of it wholy to herself.

Altemira's Letter she gave to one of her Footmen, with an Order to bring it in when she called for Tea; and to say [if any Questions were asked] a Man on Horseback enquired for my Lord, desired that it might be delivered to him, and rode away.

Amoranda desired *Formator* and *Altemira* to go up into the Room over the Summer-house, where *Brown* heard all *Calid*'s and *Froth*'s Contrivance, and where they might hear what she said to my Lord, for in the Summer-house she intended to entertain him. They were no sooner placed in their different Posts, than they heard the Visiting-Knock, and my Lord enter'd, and enquired for *Amoranda*, whom he found in the Summer-house: he ran to her with eager Transport, and finding her alone, thought Opportunity had joined itself to his Desires, and he had nothing to do but reap a Crop he never intended to make a Title to. My dearest *Amoranda*, said he, how shall I return this Favour? With what Joy did I receive your obliging Letter? And with what Delight am I come to die at your Feet? My Lord, said *Amoranda*, you seemed so very earnest in your Letter for an Interview, I was resolved to give you an Opportunity, and shall now be glad to hear what you have to say. To say, my Angel! said he, Can any Man want a Theme, that has so glorious a Subject as *Amoranda*? Come to my Arms, my lovely Charmer, and let me whisper out my very Soul upon thy lovely Bosom. Hold, my Lord, said she, before you run into those Violent Raptures, let me know your Designs a little; I confess you have often rallied a Married State, but that I rather take to be a sort of a Compliance to a Debauched, Wicked Age, than any real Inclination of your own, come my Lord, confess you have a Mind to marry. To tell you Madam, I have a Mind to marry, is to tell you, I have not a Mind to love you, why should you desire to subject yourself to one, whom you may for ever make your Slave? The very Thoughts of being bound to love would make me hate. And take it from me, as a very great Truth, Every Man breathing makes a better Lover than Husband. Pray my Lord, said she, from whence do you prove your Assertion?

tion? I muſt own, my Experience and Obſervations are but young, and yet I know ſeveral married People, who in all Appearance love one another exceedingly well.

Yes Madam, ſaid he, in all Appearance, I grant you, but Appearances are often falſe. Why then, ſaid *Amoranda*, by the ſame Rule, we may believe the Love of one of you to your Miſtreſs, as forced and empty, as that of a married Man to his Wife; we have no Way to know either but by their Words and Actions, and thoſe that think contrary to both, we look upon with ſo much Contempt, that we ſhun their Converſation, and think it a Fault to be ſeen in their Company.

What a Pity it is, ſaid my Lord, ſo many good things ſhould be ſaid upon ſo bad a Subject. I wonder, ſaid *Amoranda*, your Lordſhip does not get the Houſe of Lords to endeavour to repeal the Law of Marriage? Why ſhould you Lawgivers impoſe upon other People what you think improper to follow yourſelves? Oh! Madam [ſaid the Peer] there are Politick Reaſons for what we do; but if ever you would oblige me in any thing, let us have no more of Marriage. Why really my Lord, ſaid *Amoranda*, I am not yet at my laſt Prayers, ſo that I hope, you will not think Deſpair has any Hand in what I have ſaid; and to divert the Diſcourſe, we will have a Diſh of Tea. Here ſhe rung a Bell, and called for the Tea-Table, which was immediately brought, and followed by a Servant with a Letter for Ld *Lofty*, who no ſooner caſt an Eye upon the Superſcription than he knew the Hand to be *Altemira*'s. The Effects of a conſcious Guilt immediately ſeized the whole Man, his Tongue faulter'd, his Cheeks glow'd, his Hand trembled, and his Eyes darted a wild Horror, when ſtriving to recover himſelf, he put the Letter into his Pocket, and with a forced Smile ſaid, A Man had better have a Wife itſelf than a Troubleſome Miſtreſs. Nay, my Lord, ſaid *Amoranda*, if that Letter be from a Miſtreſs I am ſure you are impatient to read it, I will readily diſpenſe with all Ceremony, and beg you will do ſo. Madam, ſaid he, the fooliſh Girl from whom this comes, I own, I once had an Intrigue with, but——

I don't

I don't know how it was, she had a better knack at getting a Heart than keeping it; besides, she gave me such a consumed deal of Trouble, that I was almost weary of her before I had her. No my Charmer, said he, *Amoranda*, and only *Amoranda* commands my Heart, I own no Mistress but her, nor will I ever wear any other Fetters than those she puts me on. Now do I most steadfastly believe, said she, that you have said as much a Thousand Times to the very Lady whose Letter you have in your Pocket: Come my Lord, said she, either read it while I am by, or I will go away to give you an Opportunity.

Madam, said he, rather than lose one Minute of your Company I will do Penance for three or four; but be assured, I intended to have return'd it unopen'd, as I have done several from the same Hand; but to oblige you I'll read it. While he was doing so, *Amoranda* watch'd his Looks and found a fresh Alteration in his Face at every Line he read. but when he came to that part which told him, *Altemira* had recovered his Contract, he turned pale as Death, stamp'd, and cry'd—— Zouns——Bless me, said *Amoranda*, What is the Matter My Lord? Is the Lady not well? My Lord, after he had paused a while said, he was mistaken in the Hand, that Letter came from his Steward, with an Account of a very considerable Loss he had.

Pugh! said *Amoranda*, is that all? You know, my Lord, there are Misfortunes in all Families, as Sir *Roger de Coverly* says; come, come my Lord, drink a Dish of Tea, and wash away Sorrow. My Lord sate very moody for some time considering, that since *Altemira* had recovered his Bond and Contract she would, if only to revenge his ill Usage of her, be very troublesome. And again he thought, if once the World should come to see them, every body would say, he was a Villain if he did not marry her. He therefore resolved to put a stop to her Expectations, by marrying of *Amoranda*, and then she would be glad to come to his Terms, and for her own Credit smother the Matter. This was just as *Amoranda* expected, and hoped for; she wisely imagined, that if my Lord once saw himself under

under a sort of Necessity of Marrying, he would be for chusing the least Evil [as he thought all Wives were] and rather marry a Woman he had not enjoy'd, with as fine an Estate as he could expect, than take one with an inferior Fortune, and of whom he could expect no more than what he had had already. *Amoranda* saw the Struggles of his Soul in his Looks, how unwilling he was to come to a Resolution so much against his Inclinations, but he had just promised her he would wear no Fetters but what she put him on, and she was as firmly resolved to fit him with a Pair.

My Lord, said *Amoranda*, your Tea will be cold, I wish I were worthy to know what weighty Affair employs your Thoughts?

A weighty Affair indeed Madam, said he, for I am now bringing myself to a Resolution of doing what I have often thought no Woman upon Earth could have had the Power of persuading me to. But your Charms have dissolved every Design, and I now offer you a Heart for Life. My Lord, said *Amoranda*, a Man of your Estate and Quality leaves a Woman no Room for Objection, but if I should comply too soon, you will think I am too cheaply won, and value me accordingly. Madam, said he, I am one of those who hate Trouble, and the less you give me, infinitely the more you will engage me to you: Come my *Amoranda*, said he, your Old Crabbed Guardian is now from home, and there is no time like that present, I will send just now for my Chaplain, and we will do in Half an Hour what I hope we shall never repent of. But my Lord, said she, the Canonical Hour is past, and you have no Licence. The Canonical Hours, Madam, said he, are betwixt Eight and Twelve, and not a Farthing Matter whether Morning or Night, and for a Licence, I will step home myself, and take Care of one. My Lord just remembered he had one by him, which he had purchased to bamboozle poor *Altemira*, and since he was in such Haste, it was no more than scratching out one Name, and interlining another, whipt into his Coach, bid his Coachman be at home in Half an Hour, and told the Lady, in another he would be back. *Amoranda da* called down her two Prisoners, who had been within hearing all this while, and leaving them in the Summer-house, she ran in, called for a Pen and Ink, and wrote thus to my Lord:

I AM, my Lord, *in such Confusion, I have hardly Time to write to you:* Formator *is just come home, I know he hates you, and will certainly prevent our Designs, till he has wrote to my Uncle. I therefore desire you will, with your Chaplain, come, as you once proposed, into the Grove your own Way, and when it is dark I will come to you. I doubt not but your Chaplain has the Matrimony by Heart, if not, pray let him con his Lesson before he comes*

Yours in great Haste,

AMORANDA.

When she had sent this Letter Whip and Spur after my Lord, she returned to the Summer-house, and desired *Altemira* to come in, and dress her in the same Gown she had on, for though it was now past Nine o'Clock, it was light enough to distinguish Colours. As soon as they had got ready they went to the Grove, and *Amoranda* placed *Altemira* just where my Lord was to enter, and bid her whisper, under Pretence of *Formator*'s being in the Garden, as well to disguise her Voice, as to pronounce her own Name without being fairly heard; and when you are married, said *Amoranda*, tell my Lord, you will go in and go to Supper, and as soon as you can conveniently get to Bed, and send *Jenny* to conduct him to you. She here told them, she had writ to retard his Return till it was dark, and now *Altemira*, said she, I hope you are near that Happiness you have so long wish'd for: I think I hear the Coach. *Formator* [who was all this while with them] and I will place Ourselves where we shall hear you, if you speak never so low; but you shall see no more of us till my Lord is in Bed with you, and then we will come in, and wish you Joy. As soon as *Amoranda* had

done

done speaking my Lord came, and found *Altemira* ready, whom he took for *Amoranda*; the Chaplain soon did the Work, and made them One, to the unspeakable Joy of the Bride. She observed all *Amoranda*'s Orders, and whispering told him, she would go in, and send *Jenny* for him, as soon as she had an Opportunity. My Lord sent away his Coach and Chaplain, and waited with the greatest Impatience for *Jenny*, who came after some time, and convey'd him in the dark to *Altemira*. As soon as my Lord was gone out of the Grove, *Formator* and *Amoranda* came out too, who durst not stir till he was gone for fear of being heard; when they thought he was in Bed, they went into the Chamber with each a Light in their Hands, to wish the Bride and Bridegroom Joy. *Formator* went in first, and when my Lord saw him, he thought he was come to take away his Spouse, and cry'd out, Be gone Sir, she is my Wife. Fear not my Lord [said *Amoranda* behind] nobody shall disturb you, only we are come to wish you Joy How! Madam [said my Lord when he saw and heard *Amoranda*] Are you there? To whom have you dispos'd of me? Your Chamber-maid! No my Lord, said *Amoranda*, I scorn so base an Action, but I have given you to One who has the best Right to you; come *Altemira*, said she, sit up, and let us throw the Stocking besides, ye are both gone Supperless to Bed, and I have a Sack-Posset coming up-stairs.

When my Lord had look'd sufficiently round, and saw how Matters went, he found it was a Folly to complain, and was resolv'd to turn the Scale, and shew himself a Man of Honour at last, in Order to which, he turned to *Altemira*, and said, Can you forgive the Injuries I have done you Madam? My Lord, said *Amoranda*, I dare answer for *Altemira*'s Pardon; but who must answer for yours? Madam, said my Lord, I am at Age, and will answer for myself, and do *upon Honour* declare I am pleased with what you have done. There is certainly a secret Pleasure in doing Justice, though we often evade it, and a secret Horror in doing ill, tho' we often comply with the Temptation. I own, my Design was to wrong this Innocent Lady, but I had an

inward

inward Remorse for what I was about; and I would not part with the present Quiet and Satisfaction that fills my Breast to be Lord of the whole Creation. How great a Truth is it, said *Formator*, that Virtue is its own Reward; And who that knows the Pleasure of a good Action, would ever torment himself with doing an ill one? My Lord, said he, this happy Turn of Temper has made you a Friend, which you may one Day think worth your Notice: and now, Madam, said he to *Amoranda*, let us leave the happy Pair, and *Altemira* to tell her Lord every Incident that help'd to bring her wretched Circumstances to such a joyful Conclusion.

The next Morning my Lord sent for his whole Equipage, and carried his Lady home as became his Wife. *Formator* and *Amoranda* accompanied them to the House where my Lord had first decoy'd his *Altemira*, and as they went by call'd at *Cook*'s, who was soon informed of all the good Fortune that attended her young Lady, and told her, she had a Letter for her from her Brother, which she gave her. *Amoranda* told her Ladyship, There was no body in Company but who knew the Story of her Brother, and desired she would read it, which she did thus.

IF I burnt in an unlawful Flame for my Dearest Sister, I have quench'd it with my Blood; I no sooner miss'd you, than Ten Thousand Torments seised my guilty Mind; I sent Three Days in Search of you, but every Messenger returned without any News. I fear'd the Worst, and fell into the highest Despair. What have I done! said I, ruined an only Sister, left to my Care, who is now, if alive, destitute, and a Wanderer, and all this by an unlawful Love! Those Thoughts distracted me so, that I took up a Sword which lay by me, and struck it into my Breast; my Wound proved not mortal, and a few Days brought me an healing Balsam, for I was told where you were. I was resolved to drive out one Extreme by another, and see you no more, till I had tried my Success on a Creature superior in every Charm to her whole Sex; she listened to my Love, and I pursued it till I made the Fair One mine. And if Altemira *will but forgive what is past, I may call myself the Happiest Man in the World. You*

will

will, doubtless, be desirous to know my Choice; and to let you see I have not lessened my Family by it, know the Lady is Sister to Lord Lofty, *who lives so near* Cook *that you must have heard of him. I hope you will now return to the Arms of*

Your Repenting, Happy Brother.

Here was a new Occasion of Joy for Lady *Lofty*, and my Lord was very well satisfied they went al together to his House, and spent a few Days with them, till Col. *Charge'em* came from *London* to visit his Lordship; who no sooner saw *Amoranda* than he began to attack, nor she him than she began to parly. Which, when *Formator* saw [whose Eyes were always open to *Amoranda*'s Actions] he told her, If she pleased they would go home in the Morning. She consented, because she thought it in vain to deny, otherwise she had no Dislike to a Feather, nor did she think a lac'd Coat a Disagreeable Dress, and she could have dispensed with a little more of the Man of War's Company; but her trusty Guardian put a stop to all farther Commerce betwixt them, by ordering the Coach to be ready early in the Morning, so that they were almost half-way home before the Colonel was up, who very probably would have been for waiting upon the young Lady home. Lady *Lofty* and *Amoranda*, after a mutual Promise of an everlasting Friendship, parted with much Unwillingness, but with a Design to see one another often. As they were going home their Way lay between two steep Hills, where they met a Couple of Men masqued. *Amoranda* was exceedingly frighted, and said, she was sure they should be robb'd, but *Formator* bid her have a good Heart, and called to the Coachman to stop. He got out of the Coach, and taking a Pistol from one of the Footmen, stood at the Coach-Door on one side, while two of the Servants, by his Order, did the same at the other, and waited till the two Masques came to them. But they soon found Money was not their Errand, it was the Lady they wanted,

wanted, who had no other Guard than *Formator*, her Coachman, and two Footmen. One of them rid up, and shot the poor Coachman, who fell out of the Coach-box wounded, but not dead; the same Resolute Rogue rode up to the two Footmen on one side of the Coach, while the other engaged *Formator*, who hid his Pistol till he had his Enemy pretty near him, and then let fly a Brace of Bullets at him, which kindly saluted his Brain, and down he dropt. The other who had beat back the Footmen, seeing *Formator* an Old Man, rid round to dispatch him, and then get into the Coach-box, and away with the Lady; but he found the Old Man pretty tough, for before the Servants could come to him (who were both disarm'd) *Formator* had knock'd him down. he was only stunn'd with the Blow, but *Formator* staid not for his Recovery; he ordered the two Footmen to get the wounded Coachman into the Coach, and one of them to get into the Coach-box, and drive home with all Speed. *Amoranda* when the Coachman was shot fell into a Swoon, and continued in it till *Formator* got into the Coach; he laid her Head in his Bosom, and chafed her Temples till she recovered Her Reason no sooner returned than she enquired after his Safety. Do you live, *Formator*, said she, and have you no Wounds? No my lovely Charge [said he, transported beyond himself that he had her safe] I have no Wounds but what the Fear of loosing you gave me; the dreadful Apprehension of such a Misfortune stabb'd me in a Thousand Places. Well, said she, I am glad you are not hurt, but I wish we were at home.

That, Madam, said he, we shall be presently, we have not above three Miles to your own House. As soon as they got home a Surgeon was sent for to dress the Coachman's Wounds who was shot through the Arm; and *Amoranda* was some Days before she recovered her Fright Three Weeks were now past since she left Ld *Lofty's*, in which time *Formator* had, by a daily Application, endeavour'd to form *Amoranda's* Mind to his own liking; he tried to bring her to a true

Taste

Taste of that Behaviour, which makes every Woman agreeable to every Man of Sense. A Man, said he, of true Judgment and good Understanding has the greatest Contempt in the World for one of those Creatures we commonly call a Coquet: Levity and a light Carriage is so very despicable in a Woman, that it is not possible for the rest of her Qualities, though never so good, to attone for them; how much more does it raise a young Lady's Character, to have one Man of Sense vindicate her Conduct, than to hear a Thousand Coxcombs cry ——— Gad, she is a fine Woman, she is a Woman of Fire and Spirit? The Commendations of such Men, Madam, said he, are like the Compliment of a Dog just come out of the Dirt, while he fawns upon you he defiles your Clothes Nature when it formed you shew'd its greatest Skill, and sent you into the World so very compleat, that even Envy itself cannot charge you with one single Blemish, your Beauteous Form is all Angelick, and your Understanding no way inferior to it, a Temper mild and easy, and a Fortune great enough to satisfy the Avarice of the greatest Miser. And why, lovely *Amoranda*, must all these fine Accomplishments be eclips'd by that *Foible* of your Sex Vanity? Why have you such a greedy Thirst after that Praise, which every Man that has his Eyes and Ears must give you of course? For Heaven's sake dear Madam, said he, disguise at least the Pleasure you take in it, and receive it with a modest, careless Indifference: A Man who once sees a Woman pleased with Flattery has gained more than half his Point, and can never despair of Success while he has so good, so powerful an Advocate about the Heart he aims at. *Formator*, said *Amoranda*, were you never flatter'd when you were a young Man? I fancy you don't know the Pleasure of it, but I am resolved I will never think it a Pleasure again, because you dislike it in me, for it must be a disagreeable Quality, or you would never argue so strenuously against it. Nay, and there is another thing which will make me leave it, and that is ——— Hush, said she, I hear a Coach stop at the Door, let us go and see who is come. She ran into the Entry, and was most agreeably

ably surprized, to see two young Ladies alighting, one of whom was a particular Favourite, and had been her Companion when a Child; the other young Lady was a perfect Stranger, but she came with *Amoranda*'s Friend, and for that Reason was equally welcome. They came in a little before Supper, and *Amoranda* was exceedingly pleased she had got a Female Companion or two. When they were at Supper, and saw *Formator* sit at Table, *Arentia* [for that was the young Lady's Name] asked, If he was a Relation of *Amoranda*'s? She said he was better than a Relation, he was a Friend, and One to whose Care her Uncle had committed her. As soon as Supper was over, *Formator* left the Ladies to themselves, and he was no sooner gone than *Arentia* asked how long he had been in the Family? *Amoranda* said about six Months. He is, said she, a very good sort of an Old Man, if he were not so very wise; but the Truth is, we foolish Girls are not to be trusted with Ourselves, and he has thought me to believe we are the worst Guardians we can possibly have. Madam [said the strange Lady, whom we must call *Berintha*] if we young People give into all the Whims of the Old, we shall be so too before we have lived out half our Days, I hope Madam, we shall not have much of his Company, for of all Things I hate an Old Man. Oh! said *Amoranda*, you will like him better when you are acquainted with him, and will find him a very agreeable Companion; for all his Age, *Formator* has a Sprightliness in his Conversation, which Men of younger Years might be proud of. This Encomium of *Amoranda*'s raised a Blush in *Berintha*'s Cheeks, which she took Notice of, and laughing said, If you had not just now Madam declared your Aversion to Old Men, I should be half afraid you had a Mind to rob me of my Guardian. After some Discourse it grew late, and *Amoranda* asked the Ladies, if they would lie together, or have separate Beds? *Berintha* said she always lay alone, which accordingly she did. Next Morning, after Breakfast, *Amoranda* took them into the Garden, and there entertain'd them with the Story of *Froth* and *Callid*'s Contrivance, with every thing else which she thought

would

would divert them; but while they were in the midst of Mirth and Gaiety *Formator* came into the Dining-Room, and with discomposed Looks, walked a few Turns about it, saying to himself, From whence proceeds this strange Uneasiness? Why is my Heart and Spirits in such an Agitation? I never was superstitious, and yet I cannot forbear thinking *Amoranda* in some new Danger, there must be something in it, and Heaven, in pity to her, gives me Warning: Then after a little Pause —— I will take it, said he, and watch the lovely Charmer: I know not why, but methinks I tremble at the Thoughts of those two Women, and fancy I see her more expos'd to Ruin now than when she was surrounded with Fools and Fops. Saying thus, he went into the Garden, and walked at a Distance from the Ladies, but kept his Eye upon them; he perceiv'd the new-come *Berintha* close to *Amoranda*, one Hand lock'd in hers, and the other round her Waist: This Sight increased his Doubts, and raised his Indignation. At Dinner he watch'd her Looks, and found her Eyes almost continually upon *Amoranda*: The Sight was Death to him, his Soul was rack'd and tortur'd, and while he flung dissatisfied Looks at *Berintha*, she darted hostile Glances at him, his Suspicions grew every Day stronger, yet was he in such a State of Uncertainty, that he thought it not convenient to say any thing to *Amoranda*, till one Morning she came down before the two Ladies were stirring, and saw *Formator* walking in the Hall. She was glad of so good an Opportunity, for she had for several Days taken Notice of an unusual Melancholy in his Looks. *Formator*, said she, What is the Matter with you? What new Trouble has taken Possession of your Breast? I see a Cloud upon your Brow, and cannot be easy till I know the Occasion of it Madam, said he, the Source of my Trouble proceeds from the real Concern I have for your Welfare, which I have so much at Heart, that the least Appearance of Danger gives it a fresh Alarm. I confess myself extremely uneasy, but fear you will think me a very Whimsical Old Fellow, if I tell you, I suspect *Berintha*'s Sex, and cannot but fancy she is a Man.

I shall always, said *Amoranda*, acknowledge myself obliged to you for your great Care and Caution, but beg, my good *Formator*, that you will not carry it too far: What in the Name of Wonder could put such a Thought in your Head?

Madam, said he, Observation puts a great many Things into our Heads; you may please to remember, first, she would lie alone. Pugh! said *Amoranda*, that is what I love myself, and so may Ten Thousand more. True Madam, said he, and had my Reasons stopp'd there that would have dropp'd of course; but why so many kind Glances? so many rapturous Embraces? such loving Squeezes by the Hand, and eager Desire to please you? Eyes ready to run over with Pleasure at every Word you speak? Are these the common Marks of Respect betwixt one Lady and another?

Consider Madam, you have Youth, Beauty, Sense, and Fortune enough to bring our Sex to you in as many Shapes as ever *Jove* himself assumed, and we are always soonest surprised, when we are least apprehensive of Danger.

Formator, said she, every thing you say pleases me, because I know it comes from an Honest Heart, but you are too full of Fears, and your Zeal, and Care for my Safety makes you look at Things in a false Light: I cannot give into your Opinion for several Reasons, first, I think it highly improbable, a Person of *Berintha*'s Sense should undertake so ridiculous a Project; next, I can never believe *Arentia*, who must be privy to it, would be so base as to betray me. No, no, *Formator*, said she, there can be nothing in it, and I beg you will lay by your Fears. Saying thus, she left him, and went away to the Ladies, who, she heard, were both up. *Berintha* met her with an Air of Gallantry, and led her a Minuet, then catching her in her Arms kiss'd her with some Eagerness. Hold, *Berintha*, said *Amoranda*, Kisses from our own Sex and other Womens Husbands are the most insipid Things in Nature; I had rather see you dance, I fancy you do it very well, but can't be so good a Judge while I dance with you myself. You will oblige me, if you take a Turn or two a-

bout

bout the Room. This she proposed on purpose to mind her Step, which she found somewhat masculine, and began to fear *Formator* was in the right. Good Heaven! [said she to herself] can this be true? Is it possible *Arentia* can be so treacherous? Is there no Justice, no Honour, no Friendship to be depended on in this Vile World? Methinks I could almost hate it, and every Thing in it, unless Honest *Formator*. While she was thus musing *Berintha* ran to her, and taking her again in his Arms said, My dear *Amoranda*, What are you thinking of? Her dear *Amoranda* began now to disrelish her Embraces, and breaking from her a little abruptly said, Madam, I was thinking of Treachery, Falshood, broken Friendship, and a Thousand other Things, which this bad World can furnish us with. This Answer made both the Ladies colour, and they looked at one another with the utmost Confusion, which *Amoranda* took Notice of, and applying herself to *Arentia* said, Why Madam do you blush? Your Youth and Innocence are doubtless Strangers to all those black Things I accidentally named. *Arentia* willing to extricate herself from her Confusion said it was a Vapour. Oh! said *Amoranda*, is that all? then here is my Bottle of Salts for you, and yours Madam [said she to *Berintha*] is a Vapour too I presume: I will call for another for you, since your Distemper is the same your Cure ought to be so too. But come Ladies [said she being resolv'd to try them a little further] I will divert your Spleen with a Sight I have not yet shewn you. She then led them up two pair of Stairs, where there was a large Old-fashion'd Wrought-Bed. This Bed, Ladies, said she, was the Work of my Grandmother, and I dare say you will believe there was no Want of either Time or Stuff when it was made. No said *Arentia*, they had doubtless Plenty of both, or it had never got to such a Size; I don't believe it wants much of the Great Bed of *Ware*. Methinks, said *Amoranda*, they should bring up this Fashion again now that Men and their Wives keep so great a Distance, they might lie in such a one with so much Good-manners. I dare say, continued she, we Three might lie in it, and never touch one another,

other. What think ye Ladies, shall we try To-night? No, said *Berintha*, for my part, I never loved one Bedfellow, much less two; besides, I never sleep well in a strange Bed. The Proposal however took off some Apprehensions from the two Ladies, but confirmed the Third in her Fears.

Madam, said *Arentia*, I ventured to promise my Friend here, before we came from home, a great deal of Pleasure upon your fine River, here is a cool Day, and if it be consistent with your Inclination, we will take a Turn upon the Water this Afternoon, for To-morrow we must think of going home. *Amoranda* was not sorry to hear that, but told them she could not answer them of a sudden; for she knew they did not care to have *Formator*'s Company, and whether he would consent she should go without him she knew not.

I confess to you Madam, said *Berintha*, I had much rather want the Pleasure of the Water, than have the Plague of the Man, but hope you will prevail with him to stay at home, and let us go without him. Come Madam, said *Arentia*, it is our last Request, gratify us in this small Matter, and compleat the Favours we have already received. Well Ladies, said *Amoranda*, if you will excuse the Rudeness of leaving you a Minute, I will go and try my Guardian's Good-nature. She conducted the Ladies down again, and went to *Formator* I am come, said she, to tell you something, which will I dare say be very grateful to your Ears, my two Ladies talk of going home To-morrow, but they have a great Mind to take a little Recreation this Afternoon in the Barge, and I desire your Opinion of the Matter. Madam, said he, I am strangely surprized at your having an Inclination to go abroad with a Person you are utterly a Stranger to; you know the Water for some Miles runs by nothing on one side but Woods and Desarts, and has on the other but one small Town, suppose there should be a Trap laid for you, and you should fall into it, what Account can I give your Uncle, either of your Safety, or my own Care? I am sure *Formator*, said she, you do not think so indifferently of me, as to believe I have a Mind to be trapann'd, or that I
would

would not carefully avoid all Danger, but I cannot see how it is possible for me to be in any at this time, because I shall have all my own Servants about me, and if a hundred Baits were laid they could not reach me, unless I were to land, which I faithfully promise you I will not do. And supposing the very worst you fear to be true, and *Berintha* should prove a Man, he is neither a Devil nor a Monster to devour all before him, I wish you were to go with us yourself. No Madam, said he, I perceive my self a perfect Bugbear to them both, and would not make your Company uneasy. May Heaven have you always under its kind Protection; I shall be transported at Night, when I see you safe home again. Fear not *Formator*, said she, that Providence which knows my innocent Intentions will I hope conduct me back again. Here she left *Formator*, and went to order the Barge to be got ready, and then returned to the Ladies. Well, said she, I have ordered all Things for our long Voyage, and as soon as we have dined we will embark. Nay, said *Berintha*, let us take a Bit of any Thing along with us, and not stay for Dinner, we shall not have half Pleasure enough before Night else. *Amoranda* willing to gratify them this once, sent fresh Orders to the Barge-Men, who were ready in half an Hour, and when *Jenny*, by her Lady's Command, had laid in Wine and cold Viands, they sailed down the Water with a pleasant Gale. The Three Ladies were sate at one End of the Barge, and *Amoranda*'s Servants, six in Number, at the other, she herself was sate between *Berintha* and *Arentia*, when *Arentia* thus begun. Madam, said she, Fortune did me an early Piece of Service, in making me your Acquaintance when I was yet but a Child, I have ever since done my Endeavour to keep up Amity and a good Understanding betwixt us, and it shall be wholly your Fault if ever there be a Breach in our Friendship, but Madam, our Time is short, and there is a Story ripe for your Ear, which I must beg you will listen to, and hope you will contribute so much to your own Happiness, as to comply with the Proposals we are about to make to you, it is neither my Cousin's Inclination nor mine to

use

use Force, but something must be resolved upon in a very short Space: Nay Madam, continued she, don't look surpris'd, what I say is Fact, and so you'll find it. *Amoranda* gave a scornful Smile at what *Arentia* said, and asked her, if she thought her a Woman of so little Courage, as to be bullied into any Compliance in the midst of her own Servants. No Madam, said *Berintha*, *Arentia* has gone a little too far, give me leave to tell the ungrateful Tale, for so I fear it will prove. Why then, said *Amoranda*, do you tell it. A Fault committed by Chance or Mistake ought to be forgiven; but a wilful one we cannot so easily overlook. The poor Lady begun now to wish she had taken *Formator's* Advice, and had staid at home, for she saw nothing, either on her right-hand or left, but a resolute Arrogance in both their Countenances, however, they kept within the Bounds of Civility, and *Arentia* once more begun. Know Madam, said she, I am not going to tell you any thing but what you might be very well pleased to hear, I have a near Relation, who is a Man of the greatest Merit, a Man of Fortune and Honour; he had the Misfortune [as I fear I may call it] of seeing you once at the *Bath*, and though it be more than a Twelve-month since, he still struggles with a Passion that will master him, in spite of all Opposition. Oh! turn to your left Shoulder *Amoranda*, and behold the Wretch.

Amoranda, who guessed where it would end, look'd very serene and unsurpris'd saying, *Arentia*, if your Friend *Berintha* be a Man of Fortune and Honour, as you say he is, why has he used clandestine Means to get into my Company? Do you think, Sir [said she turning to him] I am so fond of my own Sex, that I can like nothing but what appears in Petticoats? Had you come like a Gentleman, as such I would have received you; but a Disguised Lover is always conscious of some Demerit, and dares not trust to his right Form, till by a false Appearance he tries the Lady, if he finds her weak and yielding the Day is his own, and he goes off in Triumph, but if she has Courage to baffle the Fool, he sneaks away with his Disappointment, and thinks no-body will know any thing of the Matter. *Bi-*

ranthus

ranthus [for that was his true Name] was stung to the very Soul to hear *Amoranda* so smart upon him; but was yet resolved to disguise his Mind as well as his Body, and said, You are very severe Madam upon a Slave who dies for you; but if I have done foolishly in this Action, *Arentia* should answer for it, the Frolick was her's, and it was designed for nothing else. But Madam, said he, Time flies away, and every Minute is precious to a Man whose Life lies at Stake, it is now Time to know my Doom, shall I live or die? Believe me Sir, said *Amoranda*, it is perfectly indifferent to me which you do; and if nothing will save your Life but my Ruin, you will not find me very ready to preserve it at so dear a Price. If, said *Biranthus*, you give me Cause to accuse you of Ill-nature, you half justify my Design upon you. Pray, said *Amoranda*, What is your Design? To force a Compliance with my Wishes, said he, if you refuse a Voluntary one. How [said *Amoranda* with a scornful Laugh] Will you pretend to Force, while I am in the midst of my own Servants?

Biranthus now grown desperate, told her she was too merry, and too secure; for know Madam, said he, those Servants of whom you boast are most of them my Creatures, the Slaves have sold that Duty to me which they owed to you, and therefore Compliance will be your wisest Course. Nay then, said *Amoranda*, I am wretched indeed. O! *Formator*! ——— *Formator*, said *Biranthus*, is not so near you now as he was when you were attack'd in your Coach some Weeks ago; I owe the Old Dog a Grudge for his Usage of me then, and would have paid him now, but I had try'd the Strength of his Arm, and found it too powerful for me, otherwise you had had his Company this once, in order to see him no more; but you have taken your Leave of him as it is. And are you, said *Amoranda*, one of the Villains that——— [here she fainted away] *Biranthus* was glad of so good an Opportunity of getting her Ashore, and calling some of the Men to his Assistance, they clapped Pistoles to the Breasts of the two Bargemen, who were all *Amoranda* had on her Side, and made them row to Land, just at the Side of a great thick Wood.

Wood. *Biranthus* and one of the Men took *Amoranda* up betwixt them, and carried her into it, which the Barge-men seeing prepared to follow and bring her back, but were prevented by the rest of the Rogues, two of which they knock'd over-board with their Oars, and the other they tied Neck and Heels in the Barge, then went in Search of their Lady. But *Biranthus* had carried her such intricate Ways, and so far up in the Wood, that the poor Barge-men thought there had been Horses ready for them, and they carried her quite away; however, they were resolved to stay till Night, in Hopes of her Return. In the mean time, the Devils that carried her off had conveyed her into the most unfrequented Part of the Wood, and laid her on the Grass to recover herself, but who can express the Rage, Despair and Grief, which appeared in her lovely Eyes, when they opened to such a Scene of Sorrow, when she saw herself in the full Power of a Threatening Ravisher, her own Servants aiding and assisting him in the midst of a Wild Desart, where nothing but Air and Beasts could receive her Cries? Oh! *Amoranda*, said she, Wretched *Amoranda*! What Sullen Star had Power when thou wert born? Why has Nature denied us Strength to revenge our own Wrongs? And why does Heaven abandon and forsake the Innocent? But Oh! it hears not my Complaints.——— Oh! *Formator*! Did you but know my Distress you would come to my Relief, and once more chastise this Odious Impudent Ravisher Oh! Wretched me! What shall I do? *Arentia*, who had been a long time silent, and confounded at her own Baseness, went to her, and said, Why *Amoranda*, do you think yourself wretched? It is in your own Power to be very happy, if you will but hearken to your Friends, and be ——— Peace, Screech-Owl, said *Amoranda*, thy Advice carries Poison and Infection in it, the very Sound of thy Words raises Blisters on me, so venemous is the Air of thy Breath. Oh! Madam, said *Arentia*, we shall find a Way to humble your Pride, and since you are resolved to make your Friends your Enemies, take the Reward of your Folly. Saying thus, she went away, leaving *Biranthus* and her own

Man

Man with her, to execute their abominable Designs against her. When she was gone the Hated *Biranthus* came to her, and said Madam, if you will yet hear my Proposals, I am now in a Humour to make you very good ones; but if you refuse them, you may expect the worst Usage that can fall to your Share, and I shall please myself, without any manner of Regard to your Quality or Complaints. It is true, my Estate is not a great one, but yours joined to it will make it so, and you shall find me in every thing such a Husband——. As I, said she, no Doubt, shall soon wish hang'd: No, base *Biranthus*, if Providence had designed me a Prey for such a Villain, I should have fallen into your first Snare, but I was delivered from you then, and so I shall be again: Before I would consent to be a Wife to such a Monster, I would tear out the Tongue by the Roots that was willing to pronounce my Doom I would suffer these Arms to be extended on a Rack, till every Sinew, every Vein and Nerve should crack, rather than embrace, or so much as touch a Viper like thyself. Then hear, said he, and tremble at thy approaching Fate This Minute, by Help of thy own Servant, I will enjoy thee, and then, by the Assistance of my Arm, he shall do so too. Thou liest, false Traitor, said she, Heaven will never suffer such Wickedness. Just as she spoke these last Words, they heard a dreadful Shriek at a little Distance, the Voice they knew to be *Arentia*'s, and *Biranthus*, who had taken hold of *Amoranda*, let her go again, and run to find out his Partner in Iniquity, who he saw just expiring of a Sting from an Adder. He then cried out as loud as she had done, when the other Rogue run to him, and left *Amoranda* to shift for herself. She was no sooner rid of them, than she heard the Sound of Horses pretty near her, and begun to run towards them Good Heaven, said she, has at last seen my Wrongs, heard my Complaints, and pities my Distress. The Horses were now within Sight of her, and she saw a graceful, fine, well-shaped Man upon one of them, attended by two Servants, to whom she thus applied herself Stranger, said she, for such you are to me, though not to Humanity I hope; take a

G poor

poor forsaken Wretch into your kind Protection, and deliver her from the Rude Hands of a Cruel Ravisher. The Stranger looking at her said, I presume Madam, you are some self-will'd, head-strong Lady, who, resolved to follow your own Inventions, have left the Care of a tender Father, and ramble with you know not who. Oh! Sir, said she, some part of your Guess is true, but Father I have none Nor Mother? said the Stranger, nor Guardian? Nor Mother, said she, but a Guardian, a good One too, I have; and were I but once again in his Possession I would never leave him while I live.

Well Madam, said the Gentleman, I am sorry for you, but am no Knight-Errant, nor do I ride in quest of Adventures, I wish you a good Deliverance, and am your humble Servant. Saying thus he and his Servants rode away. Poor *Amoranda* followed them as fast as she could, and still with Prayers and Tears implored their Pity; but they were soon out of Sight, and the loath'd *Biranthus* again appeared, coming in full Search after her, and designing to drag her to *Arentia*'s Corps, there to satisfy his beastly Appetite, and sacrifice her to her Ghost. He found the poor Forlorn half drowned in her own Tears, pulling off her Hair, and wringing her lovely Hands, calling *Formator*, Oh! *Formator!* Where are you? *Biranthus* rudely seized her on one side, and her own Man on the other, and was dragging her along, when her shrill Cries filled the Air, and reached the Ears of the Gentleman, who had just left her, and now returned again. Villain [said he to *Amoranda*'s Man] unhand the two Ladies. Sir, said *Biranthus*, there is no Harm designed against her; but the Cause of this Lady's Cries proceeds from her Concern for the Death of her Sister, who is just stung to Death by an Adder.

Oh! gentle Stranger, said *Amoranda*, believe him not, this very Creature who has now spoken to you is a Man disguised, and is going to murder me Oh! as you hope for Happiness, either here or hereafter, leave me not. Sir, said *Biranthus*, her Trouble has distracted her, do but ride forty Paces further, and you shall

shall see the poor Lady lie dead. Lead on then, said the Stranger. When they came to the Place where *Arentia* lay dead, the Gentleman look'd at her, and shak'd his Head, saying, How does Vice as well as Virtue reward itself! But Madam, said he to *Biranthus*, if those two Ladies were Sisters, what Relation are you to them? None, none, said *Amoranda*, I have already told you he is a Man, a Monster, a Villain and a Murderer; this very Man, Sir, said she, set upon my Coach about a Month ago, shot my Coachman, and would have carried me away then, but I had my Guardian with me, my Guardian-Angel I may call him, and he preserved me that time. The Rogue, when he thought he had me sure, confessed he was a Man and therefore for Heaven's dear sake take me from him, though you throw me into the River when you have done. No Madam, said the Stranger, you look as if you deserved a better Fate than that; Here, said he to his Servants, alight, and set this Lady behind me but *Biranthus* stepp'd between, and pulling out a Pocket-Pistol discharged it at the Stranger, but miss'd him; which exasperated his Men so much, that one of them run him quite through the Body. When *Amoranda*'s Man saw him fall, he ran away as fast as he could, but was soon overtaken and brought back. *Amoranda*'s Good-nature, as well as Gratitude, put her upon making Ten Thousand Acknowledgments to her kind Deliverer, and begg'd of him to finish the Obligation, by conveying her safe to her Barge. Madam, said he, I will wait upon you where-ever you please to command me, but how shall we find the Way out of this Wood? Sir, said one of his Men, I know the Way to the Water-side. Upon which he and his Companion went before, with *Amoranda*'s Man bound with a Saddle-Girth, till they came to the Barge. As soon as the two Barge-men saw their Lady come again they set up a loud Acclamation of Joy, and she got in again with the Stranger, who gave his Horse to his Servants, and they rode by the Barge till it was just at home. When *Amoranda* was set down, at her first coming into the Barge, she asked the Barge-men, What that was that lay in a Lump at the other End? That Madam, said the Men, is one of our Rogues, who we have tied Neck and Heels, And where, said she, are the other Two? Why Madam, said they, we could not persuade them to be quiet, but they would needs go and help to carry your Ladyship away, and so we knock'd them down with our Oars, and they fell plum into the Water, we ne'er thought them worth diving for, but e'en let them go down to the Bottom they will serve to fatten the Salmon. Well, said *Amoranda*, take this other Rogue, and tie them Back to Back, but set his Neck at Liberty, that part will have enough of the Halter, when he comes to be hang'd. As they were going home, the Stranger asked *Amoranda* how she came into the Wood, and in such Company? She briefly told him the whole Story; and Sir, said she if you will but land, and go in with me, you shall receive Ten Thousand Thanks from as good an Old Man, as you ever saw in your Life Madam, said the Stranger, I have had your Thanks, which is more than a double Recompence for the small Service I have done you, and after that, all other will be insipid Pray Sir, said *Amoranda*, Will you satisfy me in one Point? You seem now to be a very good-natur'd Man, why were you so cruel to me, when I first made my Application to you in the Wood? Madam, said he, there is a Mystery in that part of my Behaviour, which you may one Day know, for I hope this will not be the last Time I shall see you, however, to mend your Opinion of me, I will tell you, I left you with a Design to return, and went no farther than behind some Trees, from whence I saw you all the Time They now began to draw near home, and after some other Discourse, perceived the House When they were almost at the Landing-Sairs, the Stranger desired *Amoranda* to let her Men touch the Shore, that he might again take Horse, his Servants being just by, but she pressed him very much to go in with her, which he modestly refused, but promised to do himself the Honour of seeing her in a little Time. When the Barge-men had landed him, he gave each of them Five Guineas, for their Fidelity to their Lady, and standing on the Shore till he

saw

saw the Lady land, with a graceful Bow to her at parting, he mounted his Horse, and she, to return his Compliments, stood and look'd after him, as far as her Eye could reach him. When he was quite out of Sight she went in, calling to *Formator*. But *Jenny* came to her Lady, and told her, he went to walk in the Fields, just when she went upon the Water, and they had not seen him since. But Madam, said *Jenny*, Where are the Ladies? Oh! *Jenny*, said *Amoranda*, my Spirits are too much worn out with Fatigue and Fear, to answer you any Question; I must repose myself a little, and when *Formator* comes in let me know, for I have a long Tale to tell that good Old Man; in the mean time bid the two Barge-men *Saunders* and *Robert* take Care of their Charge. Here she went to her Chamber, and with a grateful Heart thanked Heaven for her Deliverance, but the Agent it had employed ran strangely in her Head. From whence [said she to herself] could he come? He is a perfect Stranger here-about, and how he came into that Wood, which is no Road, and at such a needful Time, I cannot imagine. Sure, Providence dropp'd him down for my Safety, and he is again returned, for he is too God-like to be an Inhabitant of this World, something so very foreign to what I have observed in the rest of his Sex, a *Je ne-scay-quoy* in every Word, every Action he is Master of ——— But what did he mean, when he said his Behaviour had a Mystery in it? Will he come again? ——— He said he would, and tell me this mighty Secret; I wish he may keep his Word, methinks I long to see him again; ——— but then, *Formator*! ——— What of *Formator*? He will not find a Fault where there is none. *Formator* is strict, but then he is just, and will not take away Merit, where he sees there is a little to it.——— I wonder what Love is, if ever I felt its Pleasure or its Pain, it is now. Those Reflections, and her wearied Spirits lull'd her to sleep, and her disturbed Mind had an Hour's Rest. When *Jenny* had laid her down, and observed something very extraordinary in her Looks, she made all the Haste she could to go to the Barge, for Information from thence, but as she was going, she met

Saunders and *Robert* at the Back-door, dragging in two more of her Fellow-Servants, pinion'd down with Cords. Mercy upon us, said *Jenny*, What is the Matter?

Aye, quoth *Robert*, Mercy is a fine Word, but if there be any shewn here, I think we deserve none Ourselves Why don't you tell me, said *Jenny*, what the Matter is? Matter! said *Saunders*, Aye, Aye, if such Rogues must go unpunish'd, for my part I'll never take Five Guineas again for being honest. Why, what the Devil have they done, said *Jenny*? Done, said *Robert*, Nay, nay, they have done, and had like to have undone, but the Man has his Mare again, and so there is nothing done to any purpose, thank Fortune. Pox take ye both, said *Jenny*, if I don't fit ye for this, may I always long in vain, as I do now, ye couple of Amphibious Rats, I'll make ye tipple in the Element ye are best used to, till ye burst your ugly Guts, before ye shall ever wet your Whistles with any thing under my Care Say you so, Mrs. *Jane*, said *Saunders*, then you shall swim in a Dike of your own making, before you ever come into my Barge again You think, Forsooth, because the Butler's your Sweet-heart, no-body must come within Smell of the Ale-Cellar without your Leave, but I-cod, your flat Bottom shall grow to the Cricket in the Pantry, before it shall ever be set on a Cushion in my Barge again You may go, said *Jenny*, and hang yourself in your Barge, it is as good there as any-where else, you great Flounder mouth'd Sea-Calf. While they were in this warm Discourse, *Formator* came in, and asked *Jenny*, If the Ladies were yet return'd? My Lady, Sir, said *Jenny*, is return'd, but no-body is come with her but the two Barge-men, and a couple of the Footmen with Ropes about them, in the wrong Place I suppose Where, said *Formator*, is your Lady? Gone to Bed Sir, said *Jenny*, but order'd me to let her know when you came in, I hear her ring just now *Amoranda* was not long coming down, when she heard *Formator* was come in, but meeting him with the greatest Pleasure, said ——————— Oh! *Formator*, I am glad we are met again, I will always allow you a Man of
deep

deep Penetration, and a discerning Judgment; come, said she, let us go and sit down in the Parlour, and I will tell you such a Story—— You little think what a fiery Tryal I have gone through since I saw you. When they were set, Madam, said *Formator*, I fear you have been frighted, you look very pale, and yet I think we have had no Winds to-day; but where, continued he, are the Ladies? Ladies, said *Amoranda*, the Monsters, the Fiends, you should have said; but they have received the just Reward of their Wickedness, and are now no more. What, said *Formator*, are they drown'd? No, said she, I'll tell you their Catastrophe; so she began, and told him the whole Story; but when she came to that part where the Stranger was concern'd, she blush'd, and sigh'd, saying, Oh! *Formator*, had you seen the Fine Man, how graceful, how charming, how handsome—— Pugh, I think I'm mad, said she, I mean how genteel he was; I'll swear, *Formator*, said she, now I look at you again, I think the Upper-Part of your Face like his, and there is some Resemblance in you Voices too, but that you speak slower, and have a little Lisp.

Madam, said *Formator*, I prophesy, I shall not be lik'd worse for having a Resemblance to this fine Man, but beg you will have a Care, he is a Stranger, as well as *Brianthus* was, and for ought you know, may be as great a Villain. Oh! 'tis impossible, said *Amoranda*, if he be bad, the whole Race of Mankind are so. No, *Formator*, Probity, Justice, Honour and good Sense, sit triumphant on his fine Face.

Madam [said *Formator* smiling] 'tis well if this Gentleman has not made a greater Conquest than that over your Ravisher, but how can you forgive his Cruelty, in riding away from you when you were in such Distress? I told him of it said she, in the Barge, and he said, It was a mysterious Action, which I should know more of another time. What then, said *Formator*, he intends to visit you, I find? He said he would. Do you think he will keep his Word, *Formator*? said she, No Doubt on't Madam, said he, a Man of so much Honour, as you say he is, will never make a Forfeiture of it, by Breach of Promise to a fine Lady. I remember, *Formator*, said she, you told me some time ago, that a Woman's Conduct, vindicated by one single Man of Sense, was infinitely preferable to a Thousand Elogiums, from as many Coxcombs. I have now brought myself to an utter Contempt for all that part of our Species, and shall for the future, not only despise Flattery, but abhor the Mouth it comes from.

I own, *Formator*, the Ground-work of this Reformation in me came from those wholesome Lectures you have so often read to me, but the finishing Stroke is given by my own Inclination. I believe it, Madam, said he, by your Inclination for the Stranger, who [that he may prove worthy of you] I wish may deserve as well in the Eye of the World, as he seems to do in your own. Well *Formator*, said she, I find you think I am in Love, and for ought I know so I am, for I am sure I feel something in my Heart that was never there before; but this I here promise you, I will never marry any Man, who has not your Approbation, as well as mine. Why then, Madam, said he, in Return for your Good-nature, be assured, I will bring my Opinion as near yours as I can, and doubt not but they will meet at last. But Madam, said he, what must be done with the two Rogues yonder? I know not, said she, I think 'tis best to pay 'em their Wages, and turn 'em off. Yes, said *Formator*, off a Ladder if you please, should we take no more Notice than that, every Rascal who has Twenty Guineas to bribe a Footman, may come when he pleases. No Madam, they must swing for Example. I own, said *Amoranda*, they deserve it, but I am not willing to take their Lives, perhaps, a little Clemency may reclaim them. Madam, said he, the Mercy you would shew them is highly becoming your Sex, but you forget 'tis doing the World, as well as yourself a Kindness, to rid both of a Villain, I therefore beg Leave to send them To-morrow Morning to the County-Jail. Then do what you will, said she, I leave it wholly to you. Next Day at Dinner *Amoranda* look'd very grave, and *Formator* very gay. Madam, said he, I begin to fear you are really in Love, else,

where

where are all those pleasant Airs? That Vivacity in your Eyes? The Smiles that used to sit upon that Fine Mouth? And the Sprightly Diverting Conversation, so Agreeable to all that hear'd it? I think, said he, we must send a Hue and Cry after your Deliverer, in Order to recover your Charms.

I believe, *Formator*, said she, what I have lost you have found, methinks you rally with a very gay Air, I am glad to see you grow so cheerful but why should you impute my Gravity rather to Love, than to the late Fright and Disorder I have been in? Do you think a Danger like mine is to be forgotten of a sudden? While they were in this Discourse, a Servant came in with a Letter for his Lady, and said, the Messenger staid for an Answer. *Formator*, said *Amoranda*, you shall give me Leave to read it, which she did, as follows.

MADAM,

THE Raptures I have been in ever since Yesterday, at the Thoughts of having served you, has deprived me of a whole Night's Sleep: What Pleasure can this World give us, like that of Obliging a Fine Woman, unless it be that of her returning it! But, as that is a Blessing I do not deserve, it is likewise what I dare not hope for, because my Wishes are superior to any Service I have, or can do. Believe me Madam, I aim at nothing less than Your Lovely Person, and wish for nothing more. Oblige me with one Line, to encourage a Visit, and if I can but make myself acceptable to You, Formator *and I will talk about the Estate.*

Yours,

ALANTHUS.

While *Amoranda* read this Letter, *Formator* watch'd her Eyes, in which he saw a pleasing Surprise. When she had read it, with a quite different Look from that she had all Dinner-time, she said, I have seen this Hand before,

before, but cannot recollect where: Here *Formator*, said she, I find you are to be a Party concern'd, pray read it, and tell me whether I shall Answer it. When he had read it, he return'd it, and said, I fear, Madam, my Advice will have but little Force: however, since you condescend to ask it, it is but Good-manners to give it. And I think you ought to have a Care how you converse with a Man, for whom you seem to have a tender Concern already, till you know something of his Circumstances.

Nay *Formator*, said she, that's the Part you are to look after, you know I have nothing to do with that, but I think there can be no Harm in one Visit, and it would be a poor Return for saving my Life and Honour, to deny him the Satisfaction of a Line: but I will write but a little, and you shall see it when I have done. She went to her Closet, and wrote the following words.

I *Confess myself so greatly Obliged by the Generous* Alanthus, *that it is not possible for the little Instrument in my Hand to make a suitable Acknowledgment for what I have receiv'd; but beg you will accept in part, of what it can do, and expect the greatest Addition from a Verbal Thanks, which is in the Power of*

AMORANDA.

As soon as she had done, she brought it to *Formator*, and when he had read it, she sealed it up, and call'd for the Messenger, whom she had a Mind to pump a little. Friend, said she, I have wrote a Line to your Master, but you must tell me how to direct it.

Madam, said he, it can never lose its Way, while I am its Convoy, I'll undertake to deliver it safe. How many Miles, said she, have you rode To-day? That, Madam, said he, I cannot readily tell, for I called at several Places wide of the Road. Was your Master born on this side of the Country? said she. I am very unfortunate, said the Fellow, that I cannot answer any of your Ladyship's Questions directly, but really, Madam,

dam, he was born before I came to him. May be, said *Amoranda*, you don't know his Name neither. Yes Madam, said he, mighty well, and so does your Ladyship doubtless, for my Master always writes his Name, when he sends a Billet to a fine Lady. I fancy, said *Amoranda*, your Master's a Papist, and you are his Chaplain in Disguise, for you have all the Evasions of a Jesuit. No Madam, said he, I have only Religion enough for one, I want the cunning Part, but Madam, said he, my Master will be impatient for my Return, so beg your Ladyship will dismiss me. Here then, said she, take that Letter for your Master, and there's something for yourself, and be gone as soon as you please.

Formator stood all this while at the Window leering at them, and laughing to hear the Dialogue betwixt them Well, Madam, said he, I am sure you are pleased, your Looks are so much mended. Pugh! said she, I think I have the foolishest Eyes that ever were, they can't keep a Secret; but they can tell you no more than I have done already. I have own'd to you, I do like this Man, who calls himself *Alanthus*, much better than any I ever saw before, and am fully determin'd to die as I am, if his Circumstances will not admit of an Union between us. But I am now going to be very happy in a Female Confidant, to whom I can intrust all my Secrets. Not another *Arentia*, I hope, said *Formator*. No, no, said she, it is a grave Lady, the only Relation I have on my Mother's side: I expect her To-morrow, she will be a rare Companion for you, *Formator*, and I can assure you she is a Woman of good Sense, and a pretty Fortune I know not but we may have a Match between you, and while I am contriving for a Companion for myself, I am, perhaps, getting you a Mistress. No, Madam, said *Formator*, I have as many Mistresses as I intend to have already, but if she comes To-morrow, I think I'll go and meet her. I'll assure you, said *Amoranda*, I intend her for my Companion and Bedfellow all this ensuing Winter. Yes, said *Formator*, if *Alanthus* does not take her Place Say no more of that, said she, but I desire you will not go out To morrow, because I fancy *Alanthus* will come, and I
would

would feign have you see him. Madam, said he, I shall not want an Opportunity of seeing him; his first Visit will not be his last. *Amoranda* cannot make an half Conquest.

I declare, said she, you are very courtly, and I begin to take a little Merit to myself upon your Account; for they say, a brisk Girl makes a young Old Man. but I'll go and undress me, and by that time Supper will be ready. While *Amoranda* was undressing, she pull'd out the pleasing Letter, and while she was reading it over again, *Jenny*, with the prying Eyes of a Chamber-maid, look'd at it, and said, I wonder, Madam, what Delight you can take in that Rude, Unmannerly Letter. What do you mean, said *Amoranda*, you never saw it in you Life before? Why, Madam, said *Jenny*, is it not that you had thrown in at the Summer-house Window in the Glove? I think it is the same Hand. Aye, said *Amoranda*, and so do I too, now you put me in Mind on't; I knew I had seen the Hand before, but could not remember where. No, *Jenny*, said she, that Letter which you call rude, I now see with other Eyes, and have Reason to believe it came from a Friend. Nay, Madam, you know best how you can bear an Affront: had any Fellow sent me such a one, I would have spit in his Face the first time I saw him: Tell me I was no Angel! An Impudent Blockhead. I find, said *Amoranda*, your Lovers must be very obsequious, *Jenny*, Pr'ythee what sort of a Husband would you have? Madam, said she, I would have one that could keep me as well as you do, One that would rise to work in the Morning, and let me lie a-bed, keep me a Maid to do the Business of the House, and a Nurse to bring up his Children; and then, I believe, I should make a pretty good Wife. That is to say, *Jenny*, said *Amoranda*, If you can get a Husband that will keep you in perfect Idleness, you will be so very good, as to be very quiet; but I find you intend to take less Pains than I should do, for, if ever I have a Child, I will not think it a Trouble to nurse it, 'tis a Work Nature requires of us. Aye, marry, Madam, said *Jenny*, if I had follow'd Nature, I should have had

Children

Children long ago for some-body to nurse. But I hear the Bell for Supper, will your Ladyship please to walk down?

When they had done Supper, *Amoranda* shew'd *Formator* the first Letter, and ask'd him, if he did not think it was the same Hand which came subscribed *Alanthus*? Yes, Madam, said he, I believe it is, and how will you excuse such Plain-dealing? Oh! said *Amoranda*, you have taught me to relish it, and I have no longer a Taste for Flattery; I see 'tis nothing but Self-Interest in your Sex, and a Weakness in ours, to be pleased with it. Believe me, Madam, said *Formator*, you make my poor Old Heart dance with Joy, to see this happy Reformation in you; and I shall give a speedy Account to your Uncle, of the Advantageous Change in your Behaviour: As for *Alanthus*, I find he has made a Way to your good Opinion of him; and if I find his Estate answers, as he seems to hint it will, I will further his Amour, and try to make you happy in the Man you like.

Formator, said the pleased *Amoranda*, Do not you think I ought to have more than a common Regard for the Man who snatch'd me from the Jaws of Death and Ruin? But what, said she, can be the Reason of his concealing himself?

Madam, said *Formator*, Man is a Rational Creature, and you say *Alanthus* has good Sense, he, doubtless, has his Reasons for what he does, but when I see him, I will give you my Opinion of him more at large. It now grew late, and *Amoranda* went to-bed, but *Alanthus*, [whom she expected to see next Day] had taken such Possession of her Head and Heart, that poor Sleep was quite banish'd. The Sun no sooner got up than *Amoranda* did so too; and leaving a restless Bed went into the Garden, to try if Variety of Objects would divert her Thoughts; after she had spent some time among the Birds and Flowers, she thought she heard the Noise of Horses in the High-way, and some-body groan, she ran and called *Jenny*, who came, and they with the Gardener ran to the Summer-house, and having opened the Shutters, they saw a fine young Lady on a *Spanish Jennet*,

Jennet, in very rich Trappings, the Lady herself in a pale Wigg, with a lac'd Hat and Feather, an Habit of Brocade, fac'd with a Silver Stuff, and attended by three Servants in rich Liveries, and her Woman, all well mounted, but just at the Summer-House Window one of her Men fell down and broke his Leg. *Amoranda* had a just Compassion for the unfortunate Man, and saw his Lady's Journey retarded, but the late Attempts which had been made upon her, made her afraid to desire her to come in: However, Good-manners took place of her Fears, and she said, Madam, If you will honour me so far as to ride into the Court, and alight, my Servants shall get you a Surgeon. The Lady accepted of the Invitation, and *Amoranda* met her at the Gate; when she had conducted her in with that Respect which she thought due to her Quality, she order'd her Coach to be got ready, to carry the Servant to the next Market-Town, within three little Miles, and where there was a very good Surgeon. *Amoranda* then call'd for Breakfast, and while they were drinking Tea, and eating Sweetmeats, she kept her Eye so long upon the strange Lady, that she was almost ashamed, and thought she saw every Feature of *Alanthus* in her, only her's had a more Effeminate Turn.

Madam, said she, if I may hope for the Honour of being better acquainted with you, and that you have not resolved to make your Journey a Secret, I should be very proud of knowing your Family, and where you travel this Way. Madam [said the young Lady] I never thought any thing so troublesome as a Secret, and for that Reason never keep any. I can assure you, there is not one Circumstance of my Life worth knowing, but if it will oblige you, to answer directly to the Questions you have asked, I will briefly tell you: My Father, who has been some Years dead, was Marquiss of *W———r*; I left a tender Mother yesterday, to go in search of an only Brother, of whom I hope to hear at Lord *B———s*. He has been from us above this Half Year, and though he writes to us often, we know not where he is. Lord *B———s* is my Mother's Brother, and lives so near you, I presume, I need not name

the

the Town, but think it is not above twelve Miles from hence. And pray, Madam, said *Amoranda*, is not the young Marquis, your Brother, called *Alanthus*? Yes, said the Lady, Do you know him, Madam? I believe, said *Amoranda*, I saw him once on Horse-back, when I was from home one Day, he is a fine Man, and I think your Ladyship like him. By this time the Servants return'd, who had carried their Companion to the Surgeon, and the young Lady again took Horse, after she had refused a great many Invitations from *Amoranda* to stay a Day or two with her, but obliged herself to call as she returned, and stay a Week with her then.

As soon as she was gone, a Thousand Thoughts crowded themselves into *Amoranda*'s Breast, and as many pleasant Idea's danced in her Fancy, she well knew *Formator* would share her Joy, and therefore call'd for him, to communicate the whole Affair to him, but was told, he rode out in the Morning before Seven o' Clock and said, he should not return till Night. She despaired of seeing *Alanthus* that Day, thinking his Sister would wholly engross him; however, she was resolved to put on all her Charms both that Day, and every Day till he came, and called *Jenny* to go up and dress her to the very best Advantage. Dinner over, *Alanthus*, who had Love enough to leave all the World for *Amoranda*, came in a Chariot and two Horses, attended only by as many Footmen. She was resolved to take no Notice she had seen his Sister, or knew any thing of his Quality, but leave him wholly to himself, and let him make his own Discovery when he thought fit. She received him, however, with a modest Delight in her Countenance, and he approached her with Love and Transport. Madam, said he, if my faultering Tongue does not well express the Sentiments of my Heart, you are to impute it to that Concern, which I believe most Men have about them, when they first tell a Lady they love. But *Amoranda*, said he, if you have well consulted your own Charms, you may save me this Confusion, and believe I love you, though I never tell you so, for nothing but Age or Stupidity can resist them. *Alanthus*, said she, you come upon me so very suddenly, that I am at a Loss for an Answer; but I don't wonder you are out of Countenance at the Declaration you have made. Love is a Subject every Man of Mode is ashamed of. It has been so long exploded, that our modern Wits would no more be seen in *Cupid's* Toils, than in a Church; and would as soon be persuaded to say their Prayers, as tell a Lady they love her

Madam, said *Alanthus*, you speak of a Set of Men, who are best known to the World by the Names of Beaus and Coxcombs. I beg, Madam, you will not take me for one of that Number, but believe me a Man of a regular Conduct, one that was never ashamed to own his Maker, or to keep his Laws, and for that Reason, whenever I take a Woman to my Arms, she shall come there with the best Authority that Law we live under can give us Believe me, *Amoranda*, you are very dear to me, and I know you much better than you think I do I think, Sir, your Words are as mysterious as part of your Behaviour in the Wood was; I can very safely tell myself, I never saw your Face till then, and if you ever saw mine before, I should be obliged to you, if you would tell me where Madam, said he, a very little time will draw up the Curtain, and lay all open to the naked Eye; in the mean time, if you dare give yourself up into my Hands, you shall find I will strive to make you very happy

I dare say, said *Amoranda*, you do not expect any Hopes from me, till I know who I give them to, or think I would bestow a Heart on one, who may run away with it, and I not know where to call for't again. No, Madam, said *Alanthus*, I have a much better Opinion of your good Sense, than to expect an indiscreet Action from you, but if I convince you, my Family and Estate are equal to your own, and can procure your Uncles Consent, have you then any Objection against me? Yes, said *Amoranda*, for all your plausible Pretences and Declarations of Love, I can produce a Letter under your own Hand, in which you tell me you don't love me. Then, Madam, said he, I'll renounce my Pretensions. *Amoranda* then pull'd out the Letter,
which

which came in the Glove, and ask'd him, If that was his Hand? He said, it was, but hop'd he had not express'd so much Ill-manners in it.

Take it then, said she, and read it over: Which he did with some Emotion, then said with a Smile, I did not think, Madam, you would have thought this Letter worth keeping so long, but you have put a very wrong Construction upon it, and I design'd it as a very great Mark of my Esteem: I sent it to put you in mind of turning the right End of the Perspective to yourself, that you might with more Ease behold your own Danger. I own the Obligation, Sir, said she, but as you have that commanding Charm of good Sense, I desire you will employ it in considering how early an Excursion I made into the World, left my Father and Mother before I understood any thing but Flattery, I might have said, or loved any thing but it, and had not my Uncle sent me as good an Old Man as ever undertook so Troublesome a Task, I might have fallen into a Thousand Inconveniences. I wish he would come home while you are here, I am sure, you would like his Conversation mightily Madam, said *Alanthus*, every thing pleases me, which gives you Satisfaction; and if I can but find the Art of pleasing you myself, I have no other Wishes. Just here a Footman came in with the Tea-Table, and turn'd the Discourse, *Alanthus* drank in Love faster than Tea, and *Amoranda*'s Charms were his best Repast. She on her Side, had not so great a Command of her Eyes, but they made sometimes a Discovery of her Heart, to the unspeakable inward Content of *Alanthus* The Afternoon was now pretty far spent, and our Lover began to think of taking his Leave; but first, he told *Amoranda*, he would not press her farther at that time, for an Assurance of his Happiness, because it was the first time he had declar'd himself, but hop'd a few Visits more would make her forget the Ceremony and Formality of a Tedious Courtship, and give him a Glimpse of the only Satisfaction he was capable of He then went with unwilling Steps to his Chariot, and *Amoranda* return'd in with a pleased Countenance, and sate down to meditate upon what had passed that Afternoon,

noon; but her Soliloquies were interrupted, by hearing her Cousin *Maria* was come, whom she had been expecting some Hours, and went to meet with that Chearfulness and Good-nature, which shew'd itself in all her Actions.

My Dearest *Maria* [said she, taking her in her Arms], you have brought me what I have long wanted, a Female Friend; And now I have you, we will not part this Winter. Madam, said *Maria*, I don't want Inclination to spend my whole Life with you, but I have a small Concern at home, which will hardly admit of so long an Absence, however, 'tis time enough to talk of that a Month hence. Nay, then, said *Amoranda*, there is a Lover in the Case. I never was in a young Girl's Company in my Life, said *Maria*, but she brought in a Lover, some way or other, but Madam, I am neither young enough, nor old enough to be in Love; that Passion generally takes Place, when Women are in their first or second Spring. Now I am past one, and not come to the other. Ah! said *Amoranda*, I fancy when the Blind Boy shoots his Random-Arrows, wherever they hit they wound.

The best on't is [said *Maria* laughing] I have had the good Fortune of escaping him hitherto, and if I thought myself in any Danger, would wear a Breast-plate to repel his Force. But I have heard, said *Amoranda*, Love is such a subtil Thief, it finds a Way to the Heart, though never so strongly guarded; besides, 'tis a Pain we all like, tho' we often complain on't. You speak, Madam, said *Maria*, as if there were a good Understanding betwixt you, but I desire you will never introduce me into his Company, for I would always say with the Old Song, *I am free and will be so*. Well, well, said *Amoranda*, I have seen as bold Champions for Liberty, as you, led home, at last, in Chains, to grace the Victor's Triumph. *Cupid*'s an Arbitrary Prince, and will allow none of his Subjects to pretend to Liberty and Property. But come, said she, we'll go up-stairs, that you may pull off your Habit, and look like one of the Family. After they had sate a-while, *Amoranda* heard *Formator*'s Voice below-stairs,

and

and said to *Maria*, There is my Honest Guardian come home, we will go down to him, he is one of the Best Men upon Earth. They found him in the Parlour, to whom *Amoranda* presented her Relation, and he with his wonted Good-manners saluted, and bade her Welcome; then turning to *Amoranda* said, Madam, You are dressed exceeding gay To-night, I doubt you have had a Visiter, and am sure if you have, he is gone away in Fetters, for you look more than commonly engaging Yes, said *Amoranda*, so I have, and wonder you would go out, when I told you I expected him. I am sorry, said *Formator*, I was not here, but did not think he would come so soon. That, said *Amoranda*, must be an Affront either to him or me, for either you think my Charms are not Attractive enough, or you think him an Unmannerly Fellow, who does not know a Visit deferr'd is as bad as none : He told me *Formator*, he knew me better than I thought he did; and I could have told him, I knew him better than he thought I did : But I was resolved to give him his own Way, and said not a Word of the Matter. Why? said *Formator*, What do you know of him? I know, said she, he is a Marquiss, that his Father is dead, that he has no Brother, and but one Sister; that ——— How Madam! [said *Formator* in the greatest Surprize] Do you know all this? Did he tell you so? No *Formator*, said she, he did not tell me so, but One did that knows as well as himself: His Sister rode by To-day, whom you might have seen, had you been at home, an Accident happened just at our Door almost, which obliged me to invite her in: And seeing her the very Picture of *Alanthus*, I enquired into her Family, of which she gave me a full Account without Reserve; and told me she had but one Brother, and his Name was *Alanthus*. I see, said *Formator*, this *Alanthus* has found the Way to please you, and this Discovery of his Family will countenance your Choice; but Madam, as you have found out one Secret, I must now tell you another: Your Uncle, before I left him, had provided a Husband for you, a Man of Worth, of Wealth, of Quality; and my Business was to take Care

you

you married no body else: Now Madam, if your Uncle's Choice be every way as good as your own, will you scruple to oblige him, when you cannot find one Objection against the Man? Why *Formator* [said she trembling] have you used me so cruelly, as not to tell me this sooner? Why did you let me see *Alanthus*, to whom I have given an Heart, which is not in my Power to recal? No *Formator*, said she, I will die to oblige my Dearest Uncle, but I cannot cease to love *Alanthus*. You yourself say, my Uncle's Choice is but as good as my own, and if there be an exact Equality between the Men, why am not I to be pleased, who am to spend my Days with him? And why must I be forced into the Arms of a Man I never saw?

It would be cruel indeed, said *Formator*, to force you to marry a Man you never saw, but Madam, you have seen him a Thousand Times. nay, and what is more, you love him too

Formator [said she with Tears in her Eyes] I did not expect this Usage from you, it is false, by all my Love 'tis false, I never cast an Eye of Affection towards any of your Sex in my Life till I saw *Alanthus*, and when I cease to love him may I eternally lose him And when I cease to encourage that Love, said *Formator*, may I lose your Esteem, which Heaven knows I value more than any earthly Good, and now Madam, said he, prepare for Joy, *Alanthus* is your Uncle's Choice. *Amoranda* was so overwhelmed with Delight at this Happy Discovery, that she sate for some time both speechless and motionless: At last, *Formator*, said she, you have given me the most sensible Satisfaction I am capable of, for I now find myself in a Condition to please a most Indulgent, Tender, Kind, Generous Uncle, and can at the same Time indulge my own Inclinations But still I am at a Loss for a Meaning to some of your Words Why do you say, if *Alanthus* be the Man, I have seen him a Thousand times? Madam, said *Formator*, you know there has been all along something mysterious in that Gentleman's Behaviour, but the next Visit he makes you will set all in a clear Light, and you shall be satisfied in every Particular.

Very

Very well, said *Maria*, it is no Wonder, Madam, you have been standing up for Love's Prerogative all this while, I see you are an Excellent Subject, and will fight for your Master; they say, Love is a catching Evil. I think, instead of staying all the Winter, I had not best to stay all the Week. What say you, Sir [said she to *Formator*] Is it not infectious? Madam, said he, I believe Love often creates Sympathy, but I never heard it was infectious, Love is a Passion of the Mind, which most resembles Heaven; and that Heart which is not susceptible of Love, is certainly filled with more inferior Passions. But I am an Old Fellow, and have now forgot both the Pleasure, Pain, and Power of it. No Sir, said *Maria*, I am sure you have not quite forgot it, you speak with too much Energy in its Behalf. I should laugh, said *Amoranda*, to see ye Two talk your selves into the Passion ye are so very busy about; you cannot imagine, *Formator*, with what Pleasure I should see ye both made One. Madam, said *Formator*, the Honour of being allied to you is a sufficient Reason for breaking any Resolution I have made against Matrimony, but I will certainly see your Nuptials over, before I think of my own: Beside, I fear this Lady will think me too Old for her.

No, no, said *Amoranda*, *Maria* is not very young herself, and you may have the Pleasure of going together, and no Mortal take the least Notice of either of ye. Aye, said *Formator*, there lies the Burden so heavy upon old Shoulders, we do not sink under the Infirmities of Age, but we are despised for being Old Though the Young are very generous, and willing to give us our Revenge, by being content to live till that despicable Time themselves. I don't think, said *Amoranda*, any-body despises a Person for having Sixty Years on their Backs, but because they then grow sowre, morose, censorious, and have so great a Pique against the Young, that they won't so much as remember they were ever so themselves Tell me *Formator*, said she, You that are free from the Weakness of Age, is not my Notion just? Madam, said *Formator*, Your Judgment runs in too clear

a Chana Channel, to be stopp'd by any Sediment: I have often thought Old People take the most Pains to make themselves disagreeable. For my Part, said *Maria*, I sit and tremble to hear all this, and shall do nothing to night but study how to avoid it. I once heard of a Great Person, who had One always by him, to put him in mind he was a Man; and I think it would be very convenient for us to have some-body by us to put us in mind we are growing Old that as he avoided Pride by the One, we may Folly by the Other Nay, said *Amoranda*, we live in a very good-natur'd World, that will tell us our Faults without being hired to it; I'll warrant you may meet with Ten Thousand, that will tell you for nothing you are an Old Maid Supper, and some other Chat of this kind, put an End to the Evening, and two whole Days were spent without seeing or hearing from *Alanthus*, during which Time *Amoranda* was very uneasy, and *Maria*, who should have diverted her, had seen so much in *Formator*, that she grew dull, and wanted a Comforter herself, by which we may see there are Charms even in Old Age, when it is dress'd in the Ornament of an Agreeable Temper. *Formator*, said *Amoranda*, You that are privy to all, will you tell me what new Mystery has introduced itself into the Behaviour of *Alanthus* now? Is there no End of his Ambiguous Proceedings? And must I never see the Riddle more?

Madam, said he, if you never do, I am satisfied *Alanthus* will have the greatest Disappointment, for I know he loves you with a Passion not to be match'd in Man But if we hear nothing from him by To-morrow, I will go myself for Intelligence. The Morrow came, but still no News, and *Formator*, who read a great deal of Uneasiness in *Amoranda*'s Looks, told her, he would go just then and bring her News, but as he was drawing on his Boots, a Servant from *Alanthus* brought *Amoranda* a Letter. She took the welcome Paper, and found these Words.

I Do not Complain, Dearest Amoranda, of an Indisposition which has confin'd me to my Bed, but that I am Robb'd of all my Joy, of all my Comfort, by being kept from Her I Love, from Her I Adore.

Oh! that Amoranda had but Love enough Herself to guess at mine, She would then have some Notion of those Torments, which Absence, Cruel Absence, creates in me: When I shall be able to throw myself at Your Feet 'tis impossible for me to know; but if You would hasten my Recovery, it must be by a Line from Your Dear Hand to

Your Burning

ALANTHUS.

Amoranda's Eyes soon made a Discovery of the Sentiments of her Heart, and *Formator*, who saw her Concern, told her, he would go and see *Alanthus*, and bring her better News. She waited with some Impatience for his Return, which was not till almost Night, and then he told her, It was only a light Fever, which his Physicians had assured him would go off in a few Days, and in the mean time, he would write to her every Day, till he was in a Condition to come in Person, which accordingly he did, and every Letter gave fresh Advice of his Recovery. When *Amoranda* found her Loved *Alanthus* out of Danger, as all his Letters assured her he was, she began to rally poor *Maria*: Madam, said she, you are grown strangely grave of late, I thought, for some Time, it had been occasion'd by your Concern for me, but though my Gaiety be return'd, yours is quite fled, I think Come *Formator*, said she, I don't know how far you may be concern'd in this Metamorphose; I assure you I expect a good Account of this Matter, and shall be very well pleased to say, *Here comes my Cousin* Formator. Well Madam, said *Formator*, when I

see

see you in the Arms of *Alanthus*, I faithfully promise, you shall dispose of *Formator* as you please. But Madam, said he, have you any Commands to *Alanthus*? I left two of his Servants at the Gate. No, no, said she, he's well again now; but I leave that to you *Formator*, send what Message you please. *Formator* went to dismiss the Men, and then *Maria* found her Tongue again. Madam, said she, how will you answer this Behaviour of yours to your Good-nature? To say so many shocking Things to me, before the very Man you fancy I have an Esteem for. I declare, if I were not one of the best-natur'd Old Maids in *Europe*, I should resent it past Forgiveness. Prithee Child, said *Amoranda*, don't be so foolish, why, I can't believe there is any Difference betwixt an Old Man and an Old Woman; and I dare promise, in *Formator*'s Name, if ever he marries, the Woman must speak first. I don't know how it is, said *Maria*, but *Formator*'s Intellects seem to be perfectly sound, and for his Out-side, there is nothing Old belonging to it but his Beard, and that I confess is a very queer one, as ever I saw in my Life: For I have been here above a Fortnight, and I am sure it has never been a Pin's Point longer or shorter since I came. Why really, said *Amoranda*, I have often minded his Beard myself, and I sometimes fancy the Man was born with it, for he has never shaved it since he came here, and one would think it might in that Time have grown very well down to his Waist. But I am glad to see you so cheerful again, prithee what was the Matter with you, to be so sadly in the Dumps? Why, said *Maria*, If I tell you the whole Truth, it will amount to no more than you have guess'd already; and I shall make no great Scruple to tell you, if I ever liked a Man in my Life 'tis *Formator*. I am glad, said *Amoranda*, it will be in my Power to serve you then, for you know, when I am married myself I am to dispose of him as I please: But what think you of the God of Love now, Mrs *Maria*? I think of him now, said she, as I did before, that the Distemper he flings among Men is catching; however, he has but wounded, I am not slain: And if

it

it were not for staying to be your Bride-Maid, I would fly for my Life, and leave the Place where I saw myself in so much Danger.

But the poor Lady found herself in a much greater the next Morning's Dawn, for one of the Careless Grooms had left a Candle in the Stable, which set the Hay on fire, consumed the Stables, and burnt all the Horses: And, for want of a timely Discovery, the Flames being very violent, they had catch'd hold of one End of the House; but the Family being alarm'd it was soon put out.

Formator, as soon as he heard the dreadful Cry of *Fire!* jump'd out of Bed, slipp'd on his Nightgown, and ran to *Amoranda*'s Chamber, he found her up, and in a horrible Fright, but hearing *Formator* come into her Chamber, she turned to go with him out of the House, and had no sooner look'd upon him, than her Fear gave way to the Surprize. My Lord *Alanthus!* said she, How, or when came you here? *Formator* was as much surprised to hear her ask such a Question, as she was to see him there, and clapp'd his Hand to his Mouth to feel for his Beard, which in the Fright and Hurry he had forgot. Madam, said he, I fly by Instinct when you are in Danger; but let me convey you hence, and in a safer Place I'll tell you more. As they were going down-stairs, they met several of the Servants coming to tell them the Fire was quite extinguished; upon which they return'd up-stairs, and went into the Dining-Room. It being now fair Day-light, *Maria*, who had been all this while with them, and had-had her share of the Terror which had attended the Night, seeing *Alanthus* and *Amoranda* look with some Confusion in both their Faces; began to recal her scattered Senses, and compare the present with the past. This *Alanthus* [said she to her self] is *Formator* in every thing but the filthy Beard, on which we have so lately animadverted, but I confess [thought she] it made a very great Alteration, and I'll try if I can find it out: she left the Two Lovers, and went, as she pretended, to see the Ruin'd Stables. When *Amoranda* found herself alone with *Alanthus*,

I What,

What, Sir, said she, am I to think of your being here at such an Hour, in perfect Health, and in *Formator*'s Gown, when I thought you on a languishing Bed of Sickness in your own House, or Lodgings? Must I always be a Stranger to your Intentions? Sure you have a very low Opinion of my Prudence, while you dare not trust me so much as with your Name or Family, and if I am acquainted with both, I owe my Intelligence to Chance; your Lordship will pardon me, if I resent it. Saying thus, she rose from her Seat, and was going, when *Alanthus* snatch'd her Hand, and said, My Adorable *Amoranda*, if I value myself for any Action of my Life, it is for carrying on so Clean a Cheat so long a Time, I have been these Eight Months under your Roof, and have never lain one Night abroad, have been daily conversant with you, and dined and supp'd at your Table, and yet you never saw me more than twice or thrice. While *Amoranda* was waiting for an Explication of what *Alanthus* had said, she saw *Maria* come laughing in with *Formator*'s Beard dangling at her Fingers-Ends: Here Madam, said she, *Formator* has cast his Skin, and left it me for a Legacy, for I plainly see it is all that will fall to my Share of the Man. *Amoranda* looked at the Beard, then at *Alanthus*; What, said she, do I see? Or, what am I to believe? Not my Eyes, for they have deceived me already; not *Alanthus*, for he has deceived me too. I beg, my Lord, you will disentangle my Understanding, and let me know at once who in Reality you are, while you were *Formator*, I had all the Value and Esteem for you which was due to a Good Adviser, and a Careful Guardian: when I took you for Ld. *Alanthus*, I look'd upon you as a Man of the highest Merit, as well as Quality; and the Additional Service you did me in the Wood gave you a very good Title to a Heart, which I thought you greatly worthy of; But now that you are no longer *Formator*, I have done with you as a Guardian; and till I am better satisfied you are Lord *Alanthus*, I have done with you as a Lover too. *Alanthus* was very well pleased with her Caution, but resolved to try her a little further,

before

before he gave her that Satisfaction she expected. Madam said he, was not the Authority I brought to introduce me sufficient? Did I not give you a Letter from your Uncle's own Hand, to receive me as a Friend?

Yes, said *Amoranda*, to receive you as a Guardian, not as a Lover; to receive you as *Formator*, not as *Alanthus*: And if you could so dextrously deceive me, perhaps you have done the same by him. I fear, Madam, said *Alanthus*, you would be pleas'd to find me unworthy of you, and would be glad of a fair Pretence to make me a Stranger to your Favour. No, said she, Heaven knows, to find you any thing but Lord *Alanthus*, would be the greatest Disappointment I am capable of knowing, and I have made too many Declarations to *Formator*, of my Love for *Alanthus*, to grow indifferent to him all of a sudden. But such a gross Imposition as this might prove, would not only ruin my Fortune, but call my Sense in Question too, though I confess, there is one Circumstance, which makes me hope you are the Man I wish. And that is, the Account I had from your Sister, of your Family. Nay, I have still another, which will crowd in to justify you; a Face I own you have, which says a Thousand Things in your Behalf, and reproaches me as often for my weak Suspicion of you.

Let all Disputes for ever cease betwixt us, said *Alanthus*, as I will this Hour give you Satisfaction. He went away to his own Apartment, and when he had dress'd him, returned with a Paper in his Hand. Here, my *Amoranda*, said he, let this convince you. She took the Paper from him, which she knew to be her Uncle's Hand, and found these Words:

THE *Man, my Dearest Niece, who some Months ago appeared to You as the Grave, the Wise, the Old Formator, is now turned into the Gay, the Young, the Accomplish'd Lord Marquiss of* W————, *and whenever he thinks fit to discover himself, it is greatly my Desire You use him as such. He has done me the Honour to accept of me for*

a Friend,

a Friend, and promised to make You the Partner of his Bed, if he liked You when he saw You, and could find a Means to cum Your Affections; if not, You will never know him for what he is.

When *Amoranda* had read the Paper over, she reassumed her Cheerful Looks, and Pleasure diffused itself in every Muscle of her Face. But, my Lord, said she, this Discovery being made by Chance, who can say you design'd it should ever be made at all? I can, said *Maria*, for I was so near running away with *Formator*, that my Lord *Alanthus* would have been glad to have bought himself off at the low Expence of a little Secret. Madam, said *Alarthus*, if I had design'd to have liv'd in Masquerade as long as I staid in your House, you should never have seen me as *Alanthus* at all, neither would I have staid so long with you. I came to you disguised like an Old Man, for two Reasons; First, I thought the sage Advice you stood in Need of would sound more natural, and be better receiv'd from an old Mouth than a young one. Next, I thought you would be more open and free in declaring your Sentiments of every thing to me as I was, than as I am. How good an Effect my Project has met with, you are not, I hope, insensible, and I beg you will give me Leave to remind you of the vast Difference there is betwixt your Behaviour then and now. My Lord, said *Amoranda*, I am so far from derogating from your Merit, that I own, when you first took me under your Care, I was a giddy, thoughtless, inconsiderate Mortal, fit only for the Company of those Coxcombs I too frequently conversed with. But then, my Lord, you shall own in your Turn, that I received all your Lectures and Admonitions with the Spirit of a willing Proselyte; that I was ready to give into all your Maxims, and took your Advice as fast almost as you gave it. But pray, my Lord, [said she, taking the Beard] let me once more see my Good Old *Formator*, let me once more behold you in that Dress, which so artfully deceiv'd me. Methinks I grieve

I grieve when I tell myself, I have lost the Good Old Man. Aye, said *Maria*, 'tis pity so good a Character should be a Fictitious one, but alas for me! the Loss is mine, and if my Lord assumes the Dress again, I shall certainly lay some Claim to the Man. *Alanthus* took the Beard, and dressed himself, as when *Formator*. Now, my Lord, said *Maria*, you are in the Height of all your Charms; the Grave, Sententious, Grey-bearded *Formator*, had certainly Attractives, which the Gay, Smooth-Chinn'd Lord *Alanthus* wants. In your Eyes, said *Amoranda*, remember the Fable, the Fox complain'd of Acids, when he could not reach at ———— And yet I can't but love that Form myself, when I consider the Advantages that accrued to me under its Government, the just Rebukes, the friendly Persuasions, the kind Admonitions, the assiduous Care, to turn *Amoranda* from Folly and Madness, to that Behaviour so ornamental to her Sex. Then it chastised the insolent Designs of *Callid*, and repelled the rapid Force of *Brianthus* when he shot my Coachman, and would have run away with myself. Can those Things die in Oblivion? Can they be forgotten in a Generous, Grateful Heart? No! *Formator*'s Name shall always be dear to *Amoranda*, and shall for ever find a Resting-place in her Breast. Madam, said *Maria*, You'll spend so many Raptures upon my Old *Formator*, that you will leave none for your own Young *Alanthus*. Yes, said *Amoranda*, I have one Acknowledgment to make *Alanthus*, which is equivalent to all the rest, and that is the Great Deliverance he brought me in the Wood. But now I think on't, my Lord, you promised to tell me why you left me in such exquisite Distress, when I sued for your Assistance in that Dreadful Place. Madam, said he, You may please to remember, when you suffered yourself to be drawn from your own House by those Two Impostors, it was extremely against my Liking, and I said as much as Modesty would admit of to put a Stop to your Design; but when I found, by your excusing them, you were resolved to go, I went to my Servants,

vants, who are three Miles off, got on Horse-back, and with two of them rode directly to the Wood, where I knew the Scene would be Acted, if they had any ill Design against you. I was there an Hour before I met you, and ranged about every Part of it, till I heard some Voices, and when the base *Arentia* shrieked for her Life, I heard the Cry, and thought it had been yours. I then clapp'd Spurs to my Horse, and was riding towards the Sound, when I met you. How full of Joy my Heart was when I saw you safe, I leave to every Heart as full of Love to judge; but I was resolved, if possible, to cure you, at once, of Rambling with Strangers. In order to which, I put on an Air of Cruelty, which, Heaven knows! my Heart had no Hand in, and rode from you. I knew it would give you double Terror, to see a Prospect of Relief, then find yourself Abandoned: And I likewise knew, the greater your Fear was then, the greater your Care would be for the future to avoid such Enterprizes. But I had yet a View in favour of myself, and had Reason to believe, the greater your Deliverance was, the greater Value would you set upon your Deliverer, and those Considerations carried me behind a Tuft of Trees, where I Absconded, till I saw you environ'd in the utmost Danger. Methinks, I yet behold my Trembling Fair, with lift-up Hands, and watery Eyes, imploring Help, and striving to convince me *Biranthus* was a Man, though some Hours before, I seemed ridiculous to her for only suspecting of it.

I own, my Lord, said *Amoranda*, I owe a Thousand Obligations to your Generous Care, and my whole Life will be too little to thank you for them, but ——— No more, Madam [said he, interrupting her] I had a glorious Return for all that Care, when at Night, as *Formato*, I heard the whole Story over again, and so much in Favour of the Happy Stranger, as *Jove* himself would have listened to with Envy; and if ever Vanity had an Advantage over me, it was that pleasing Minute. This call'd a Blush into *Amoranda*'s Cheeks, who

who said, she little thought when she made a free Confession to *Formator*, that *Alanthus* was within Hearing. But I have another Piece of Cruelty to lay to your Charge, my Lord. Since you had, by your Disguise, found out my Weakness, and knew I had a Value for you, why did you send me Word you were in a dangerous State of Health, when at the same time you had no Indisposition but what proceeded from your Mind, in giving me Pain when you had none yourself? My Dearest *Amoranda*, said he, pardon that one Trial of your Love, it was not possible for me to deny myself the exquisite Pleasure I knew your kind Concern would give me, but, Good Heavens! How did my longing Arms strive to snatch you to my Bosom when you had read that Letter, that I might have suck'd in the pleasing Tears which dropp'd from your lovely Eyes. Pray, Madam, said *Maria*, will you order your Coach to carry me home again? I am resolved to go into my own Country, and pick up some sweet Swain to say a few of those Fine Things to me. My Lord, continued she, will you be pleased to oblige me with that Engaging Beard of yours, that if the Man, whom Interest persuades me to, should want Exterior Charms, I may clap it on his Face, and fancy him *Formator*. With all my Heart, said my Lord, there it is, and may it contribute as much towards your Happiness, as it has done towards mine; but I believe you are the first Woman under Thirty that ever fell in Love with a Grey Beard. Aye, or over it either, said *Amoranda*, but pray, my Lord, said she, now that we have set Things in a little Order between ourselves, give me Leave to enquire after your Beautiful Sister, she promis'd to honour me with a few Days of her Company, as she return'd from Lord B————. Madam, said *Alanthus*, You saw her since I did, I have wrote to her several times since you told me she was on this side of the Country, but have not seen her yet, nor does she know where to write to me. While the Words were yet in their Mouths, *Jenny* came running in, and said,

The

The young Lady who had been here some time ago, was come again in Lord B ———'s Coach, and was just alighting. Pray, my Lord, said *Amoranda*, put on your Disguise once more, that I may have the Pleasure of seeing your own Sister as much deceived as I have been. My Lord clapp'd on the Beard, and *Amoranda* went to meet Lady *Betty* [for so she was called] and when she had conducted her in, and the common Compliments had passed, *Amoranda* told Lady *Betty*, she now claimed her Promise of staying a few Days with her Madam, said Lady *Betty*, it is that Promise that has brought me here now, and had I never made it, you had seen no more of me. For I own it was always my Opinion, that a Person who is not in perfect Good-Humour, should never incumber other People with their Chagreen, of which I am at present so very full, that you must have an uncommon share of Good-Nature, if you can bear with my Company Methinks [said *Alanthus*, disguising his Voice as usual] it is a Pity so young a Lady should have so early an Acquaintance with any thing that could ruffle her Temper, you have likely, Madam, left a Lover behind you P'shaw, said Lady *Betty*, ye Old Gentlemen always think a young Girl's Mind so set upon Lovers, that they have not Room for any other Thoughts Though he that gives me a present Uneasiness is a Lover, I hope, but he is a Brother too I remember [said *Amoranda* smiling] Your Ladyship spoke of an absent Brother last time I had the Honour of seeing you, have you never seen him since? No, Madam, said Lady *Betty*, I fancy he's got into *Fury Land*, he lets me hear from him, but will not tell me how he may hear from me; it is a little odd he should make his own Mother and Sister Strangers to his Abode Madam, said *Maria*, Has your Ladyship any Faith in *Astrology*? This Old Gentleman here is so well skill'd in the Occult Sciences, that he can in a quarter of an Hour tell you when and where you shall see your Brother; nay, I dare be bold to Affirm, he can, without stirring out of the
Room,

Room, shew Him to you in his full Health and Strength, without so much as *Raising the Devil* to help him. Madam, said Lady *Betty*, I should never have taken the Gentleman for a Conjuror, he does not look like one; nor do I believe any Man upon Earth has a Power of doing what you have promis'd in his Name, unless Lord *Alanthus* be in some Closet in this Room. No, Madam, said *Alanthus*, there is no Man in this Room but myself, and yet I believe, I could make a shift to perform all those Difficulties which the Lady has told you of. *Amoranda*, who sate next to a Window which look'd into the Court, saw a Coach and Six come in, with Servants in her own Livery. Bless me, *Formator*, said she, who have we got here? *Alanthus* ran to the Window, and saw Mr. *Traffick* alighting. Oh! Joyful Day, said he, Madam, here is your Uncle! They ran to meet him, and brought him in to Lady *Betty* and *Maria*, so full of Raptures and Tender Sentiments at the Sight of his Beauteous Niece, that his Eyes ran over with Tears of Joy; no less did the Sight of his Beloved *Alanthus* transport him: But how comes it, my Lord, said he, that you are still *Formator*? I thought by this time I should have met you with the Respect due to the Worthy Lord *Alanthus*. Lady *Betty*, at those Words, stood like one aghast, and looking round her for Interpretation, she cast her Eyes on Lord *Alanthus*, who had pull'd off his Beard, and whom she saw in her Brother's Form; but so far from running to him with the kind Caresses of a Sister, that she shriek'd out, and fell in a Swoon. For, *Amoranda* being an Accidental Acquaintance, and *Maria* a perfect Stranger, who had just been telling her, the Old Man was a Conjuror, and she not expecting to find her Brother there, and seeing him all of a sudden turned from an Old Man, whom she had never seen before, to a Brother, whom she knew not where to find, she thought herself in some Inchanted Castle, and all about her Fiends and Coblins. The whole Company quickly surrounded her, and brought her to herself again;

gain; when Lord *Alanthus* took her in his Arms, and said, Why, my Dear Lady *Betty*, are you so extremely surprised? Look round you, Madam, with Cheerfulness, and believe yourself in the Arms of your Unfeigned Brother, and among your Real Friends: This, my Dear Sister, is the *Fairy-Land* where I have so long lived *Incognito*, and there's the Inchantress, who, by a Natural Magick, has kept me all this while in Chains of Love. Poor Frighted Lady *Betty*, who had always done *Amoranda* Justice, in thinking greatly in her Favour, began to hear and believe all, and when she had perfectly recover'd her Surprise, she turned to *Amoranda*, and said, From the first Moment I saw you, lovely *Amoranda*, I had an inward Impulse to love you, and how well I am pleased with that Alliance I foresee will be betwixt us, my future Behaviour shall shew, in the mean time I beg I may be let into the whole Affair and know why Lord *Alanthus* affected the Frightful Air of an Old Man, rather than his own Faultless Form. Madam, said *Amoranda*, I hope I need not take much time to persuade Your Ladyship to believe I am very proud of your promised Friendship, and shall always with my utmost Industry strive to deserve it, but for the Scheme of the Beard, since I had no Hand in it, I leave it to be explain'd by those that had. Lord *Alanthus* and Mr *Traffick* are the fittest to give Your Ladyship an Account, which I leave them to do, while I beg Leave to go and dress me. *Amoranda* and *Maria* went to their Dressing Rooms, while the two Gentlemen entertained Lady *Betty* with the Story she desired to hear. As soon as *Amoranda* and *Maria* returned, Lord *Alanthus* went to the former, and taking her by the Hand, said, I hope, my Dearest *Amoranda*, you remember what a long time of Self-Denial I have had, and that during *Formator*'s Reign I never durst so much as touch your Hand, though my Heart had Ten Thousand Flutters and Struggles to get to you. But as we are now barefaced, and know one another; as we have determined to make each other happy, I beg you will no longer pro-

procrastinate my Joy, but let this Day, this very Day, clap us into *Hymen*'s Fetters, there to remain till Death do us part The whole Company joined in the Request of *Alanthus*, and Mr *Traffick* added a Command, which met with no Opposition. Every thing was immediately prepared, and the Nuptials solemnized that Afternoon, to the very great Satisfaction of all Parties: And after a Week more spent where they were, they all took Coach, and went to *London*; where the Reader, if he has any Business with them, may find them.

F I N I S.

Lightning Source UK Ltd.
Milton Keynes UK
UKOW06f2012130913

217186UK00012B/965/P